Relax Dad

It's Just the Kitchen

By: Stan Reese

DEDICATION

This book is dedicated to all of my test subjects.

For my wonderful wife, Valerie and my beautiful children: Shanna, Bryant, Granger, Maggie and Laina. Also for Darryl, Nonna and Papa who often enjoy my creations.

Especially for Gramsie who believed in me even when I didn't believe in myself.

TABLE OF CONTENTS

Dedication 3
Introduction 7
My Destiny 9
Don't be Afraid of the Kitchen 12
General Kitchen Tools 15
The Staples 17
A Trip to the Market 19
General Measurements, Abbreviations and Meanings 21
Safe Food Handling 23
Setting My Table 25
Breakfast 32
    SCRAMBLED CHEESY EGGS 33
    FRIED EGGS 35
    BAKED EGGS AND CANADIAN BACON 37
    BREAKFAST CASSEROLE 39
    BISCUITS 41
    MILK GRAVY 43
    BANANA PANCAKES 45
    RAISIN PANCAKES 47
    APPLE CINA-MAN PANCAKES 49
    CHOCOLATE CHIP PANCAKES 51
    CHEESY GRITS 53
    MUFFINS 55
Lunch 58
    BOILED WATER 59
    HOT DOGS 60
    TUNA SALAD 61
    GRILLED HAM AND CHEESE SANDWICH 63
    THE AUBIE DANG 65
    BURGER BURGER 67
    OAKIE SANDWICH 69
    CHEESE QUESADILLA 71
    HOGS IN A QUILT 73
Dinner (also known as Supper) 76
    BEEF ROAST WITH POTATOES AND CARROTS 77
    POTATO SALAD 79
    CHEESY MASHED POTATOES 81
    GARLIC MASHED POTATOES 83
    POTATO CAKES 85
    FRIED POTATOES WITH ONIONS 87
    SPAGHETTI 89
    SPINACH LINGUINE WITH CHICKEN BREAST AND RED SAUCE 91
    CHILI 93
    HAMBURGER STEAKS 95
    HOME MADE CHICKEN FINGERS 97
    CHICKEN AND RICE CASSEROLE 99
    PORK CHOPS 101

- MEAT LOAF 103
- BEEF SKIZZLE 105
- COLE SLAW 107
- HUSHPUPPIES 109
- CORNBREAD 111
- MEXICAN CORNBREAD 113
- CORNBREAD MUFFINS 115
- CUBED STEAK 117
- BROWN GRAVY 119
- BURRITOS 121
- TACO SALAD 123
- PO MAMA STEW 125
- SALMON PATTIES 127
- KRAUT AND WEENIES 129
- HOT WINGS 131
- BLACK EYED PEAS 133
- PINTO BEANS 135
- VEGGIE SOUP 137
- FRIED CHICKEN LIVERS 139
- BEEF LIVER WITH ONION GRAVY 141
- GRILLED STEAK 143
- FRIED FISH 145
- BAKED FISH 147

Desserts 150
- BIRTHDAY CAKE 151
- CUPCAKES 153
- SUGAR COOKIES 155

Holidays 158
- ALMOST MOM'S CORNBREAD DRESSING 159
- TURKEY 161
- STUFFED EGGS 163
- HAM 165
- FIVE CUP SALAD 167

Parties 170
- PROENZA BEAN DIP 171
- HACIENDA DIP 173
- SWEET SOUTHERN TEA 175
- PLOPCORN 177
- FRIED PICKLES 179
- SAUSAGE BALLS 181
- SALSA 183
- FLIPPIN DIP 185

And Finally 187
Acknowledgements 188

INTRODUCTION

I was the youngest of five sons, raised by traditional southern parents in Georgia. What this means is that I was spoiled. I never cooked for myself. I never cleaned for myself. That is, until I was faced with being a single parent of two small children. By this time, both of my parents had passed away and I had almost no one to look to for advice.

There was no internet. There was no support group for single dads. I had to learn on my own through trial and error- many, many errors. If someone had written this book and given it to me back then, it would have been a God-send (for me and my hungry babies). That is why I am writing it today.

Maybe you are a single man just starting out. Maybe you have kids or perhaps you are by yourself. Maybe you are just a man who wants to do better in the kitchen for his wife and family. Whichever label belongs to you, I'm sure that this book will help you become a better steward of the kitchen. It won't help you to become a French Chef but it will help you put together a few meals that just may end up enjoyed instead of thrown away.

As you read these pages keep in mind that this is just a guide. Everyone is different. The men who live in Washington State may like a different taste that those who live in Texas or Indiana or Virginia. Feel free to experiment. If one spice isn't right for your taste, try a different spice. If you need more salt or more pepper, by all means, add it. Whether it is my recipes or the recipe handed down by your grandmother, always remember that you are in charge of the ingredients. You'll have more fun that way.

Relax, Dad. Cooking is not difficult. It's simple. It just seems to be in our nature, as men, to make things harder sometimes.

MY DESTINY

My mother referred to herself as a home-maker and cooked three meals a day- I mean really started the stove and cooked the food, even breakfast. We only had cold cereal once a week and that was on Sunday morning before church.

After church, she'd grab a whole chicken and start slicing away until she had enough pieces to fry for all of us. We'd have potato salad and real biscuits with gravy and maybe even fresh green beans from the garden to go along with some real home-made fried chicken.

That's the way I was raised. I never had to even make my own sandwich. I never had to clean my room. I was spoiled and didn't know it. In college, my dorm room never got swept the whole time I was there. I had no earthy idea how to use that tool they called a dust pan and Mama wasn't around either.

I was married in 1985. We brought a daughter into the world and then a son. The wife worked sparingly and I labeled her as my own personal home-maker. I don't think she liked the label. By 1989, she went off in search of a new label and for the first time in my life, I had to cook and clean.

I had a three year old daughter and a twenty- month old son when we filed for divorce. Both of my parents were deceased, and I had little contact with the rest of my family. I got the house and the car and the kids. I didn't get an instruction booklet.

I made the rules as I went along.

For the first several months, it was hamburgers and cheesy macaroni one night followed by hot dogs and cheesy macaroni the next night. I found a few recipe books, but they were a bit too complicated for me. I soon discovered frozen dinners and, of course, happy meals.

But times got hard. Frozen dinners and happy meals just wouldn't fit into the budget. I had to learn how to cook from scratch and it scared the golden arches out of me.

My first test subjects are now grown and have their own lives so I must have done ok. I have remarried and started a whole 'nother batch of test subjects. I continue to do most of the cooking for my five year old son, four year old daughter, three year old daughter and wife. They don't complain; especially the wife.

What cooking has allowed me to do, I think, is to be a better Dad. I'm not the perfect Dad by any means but I try really hard.

My own Dad was a good dad. I never complained. We connected with sports, but we really never connected in the way I think do with my own kids.

This connection helped me to finally realize what my destiny was.

My oldest son, Bryant, had come home for a visit from college and was a few months short of a deployment with his Reserve Unit to Iraq. He knew I was worried about him. He could feel it. He figured a walk in the yard would help.

As we walked, my youngest son, Granger, ran ahead of us and I held what was then my youngest daughter, Maggie, in my arms. At twenty years old, Bryant was a confident man. I had done a good job raising him. He knew right from wrong, and he felt that serving his country was the right thing to do at this time. I wasn't so sure. He was trying his best to convince me.

Granger may not have known it then, but he was born with a good role model in his big brother.

When my wife had gone into labor with Granger, Bryant was at his high school senior prom in 2006. She gave birth to Granger the next day as Bryant was taking the ACT for college. The two brothers met later that afternoon. A star lost its brilliance at that instant because that was the day that I saw a glitter in Granger's eyes that he has always had for Bryant. They both have it.

On this particular day, however, it was more about me and Bryant. As we walked, we talked. Bryant told me he thought about making military his career after college. I joked that I didn't know, yet, what I wanted to be when I grew up. Maggie cooed. At barely a year old, she sensed how funny I could be.

And then it hit me. At forty-something years old, I finally knew what I was destined to be.

As a young child, I had dreamed of being a stock car driver when I grew up. In high school, I secretly hoped to be recruited to play football for Bear Bryant. I had been a disc jockey, a TV sports and news reporter, a cop, and even a finance and collection specialist. But, with a simple walk in yard it became clear: I was put on this earth to be a Dad.

I would have enjoyed going around the Daytona Superspeedway at close to 200 miles per hour. I would have loved to hear the roar of the crowd as I kicked the winning field goal to beat Auburn. Being a disc jockey and a TV reporter was fun. Being a cop was confusing and being in finance was challenging. I had enjoyed all of my jobs, but, for 25 years, I had always wondered what I was destined to be.

It all seemed to have lead up to this one moment for me.

When I was a sports reporter, I had the opportunity to be on the field for the first pitch before an Atlanta Braves game. I was talking with the mayor of our home town. It was Troup County night at the old Fulton County Stadium. I had just announced community night and the names of the little league teams that were in attendance over the massive public address system.

The mayor looked at me shortly after I finished and asked if I was nervous doing that with 45,000 people listening. I remarked that it didn't make me nervous at all because maybe only a dozen people were listening anyway. I told him that it makes me more nervous to talk to my kids.

He looked at me puzzled. I explained that, no matter what I say, my kids are listening and sometimes they hear learn from what I say. I told him that a slight mess-up in front of 45,000 strangers is nothing compared to messing up in front of my own kids. I surprised myself with the statement. I think I stunned him.

At the end of my walk with Bryant that day, I remembered my talk with the mayor at the stadium. I realized that, despite messing up at times, I had done well as a parent and he had done well as a son.

I told Bryant that I was proud of him. I hugged him. I told him I love him. And I smiled and admired my work.

He has since finished his tour and is back in college.

Since that walk, Granger and Maggie have now been joined by Delaina. The girls love their biggest brother, but they have that same sparkle for their biggest sister, Shanna. What a great role model she is. What great kids I have. I guess I did do ok at being a Dad. So far, at least.

I have five kids born from 1985 through 2009. I am a lucky man. I enjoy my job.

Don't be Afraid of the Kitchen

Relax, Dad, the kitchen is your friend.

I had a dishwasher for one year during the first decade after my divorce. I lived in six different houses in two different states. I always had a refrigerator although sometimes I was stood taller than the fridge. I had at least two working eyes on the stove and an oven. I had a microwave most of the time.

My kitchen was never perfect.

I not only learned to cook but I also learned to wash dishes and I learned to shop. That's the basics. If you can go to the store and buy the right ingredients, cook it and then clean up your mess, you've got it covered no matter what size or shape your kitchen is in.

I have always preferred to clean up as I cook. For instance, if I use a measuring cup, I try to rinse it and put it in the dishwasher when I am finished. If I use a pan, I scrub it in the sink and put it away long before the meal is complete. I put the salt back on the shelf and the butter back in the fridge as soon as I add the required amounts to the recipe.

When I peel a potato, I do it near the trash can so you I can toss it as I go. That goes with anything that has peelings or shells or pits or trimmings that need to be cut off.

By cleaning up after yourself as you go, you cut down on the clutter and the mess. I found that this keeps the frustration under control as well.

Then, once the meal is complete, enjoy eating the food without staring back at a kitchen piled high with pots and pans.

On shopping, I recommend shopping at the simplest store possible.

While the large mega-stores are great, the smaller stores are much less complicated. They don't have a great selection of products, but that is good, at least in the beginning. No one needs to panic in the store before they can get the food home to the kitchen.

I have learned that organic is good but expensive.

Name-brands like Heinz or Hunts or Welch's or Jiff are familiar because of all of the advertising but that same advertising makes these products more expensive. I try to buy generic when available and, if it's not great, I can buy the more expensive name next time.

I buy a lot of canned veggies but that's out of habit. Frozen is better and fresh is best.

As far as recipe books: if you have never cooked before, try the simple recipes first. Don't try to become a five-star Chef overnight.

Through the years, I have tried hundreds of recipes. I am not ashamed to say that more than a few of those have failed. One recipe in particular caused an evacuation of my apartment building.

We were living in a small town in Virginia around 1990. It was a four family apartment building. I liked my neighbors. They liked me. They didn't like it when I cooked.

I had found a recipe for a mackerel and cheese puff loaf. I liked mackerel but I loved cheese puffs. It was a lot like meat loaf so I figured I'd give it a try.

About forty-five minutes into the baking, the kids and I fled the apartment. The neighbors all seemed to follow in a less-orderly manner. They all asked the same question: "what is that smell?".

Being the honest person that I am, I acted innocent. That is until Shanna, who was five at the time, told everyone what it was. I shivered shamelessly in the cool night breeze.

Don't be afraid to try something new but, if you do, prepare an evacuation plan ahead of time…and tell your kids not to be so candid with the neighbors during highly discrete times.

GENERAL KITCHEN TOOLS

This is the part of the book that separates the men from the women. Really.

Most women know what a baster is. Most men giggle at the name. Most women are familiar with tongs. Most men waggle their tongues and think that a tong is a tiny piece of lingerie.

You don't have to be a rocket scientist to be a decent cook and you don't need a degree in languages to identify the basic tools and necessities of a good working kitchen.

When I was first starting out, I had a stove with an oven underneath, a fridge and a sink. I had a spatula and a vast array of knives, spoons and forks that had belonged to my mother. That was about it. I bought my first set of mixing bowls and thought I was the Galloping Gourmet.

Don't bust your budget on gadgets and tools. You can spend the money you save elsewhere. Below is a pretty simple list of the things you will need in order to cook basic recipes. I hope that you already have the basic stove, oven, fridge, sink and microwave. Remember, the key word is "simple".

- At least two mixing bowls, medium size
- A set of measuring cups
- A set of measuring spoons
- A two-cup measuring glass
- One good butcher knife
- Two wooden (preferably) mixing spoons
- Two large serving spoons
- Two large forks
- An set of spoons (8-10 depending on the size of your family)
- A set of forks (8-10 depending on the size of your family)
- A set of butter knives (8-10 depending on the size of your family)
- A set of steak knives (8-10 depending on the size of your family)
- Plates (and saucers and cups if needed) for at least two family meals
- Drinking glasses (plastic or glass)
- A standard can opener (electric is ok but they do break)
- A toaster
- A blender or a hand mixer (but you can always use the blender for other things like smoothies)
- One good stainless steel frying pan (I have never found a non-stick pan that I like)
- One large stock pot
- One large sauce pan
- two medium sauce pans
- one small sauce pan

- Tongs (not thongs)
- A few serving bowls (you can get some really nice antique serving bowls at the flea market)
- One cookie sheet
- One muffin pan
- Two eight-inch cake pans
- One metal and one plastic spatula
- Two pie pans (glass is ok)
- A casserole dish (glass is ok)
- A one-gallon drink pitcher
- A half-gallon drink pitcher
- One hand held grater (for slaw, onions, etc)
- One crock pot
- One electric skillet
- A George Forman grill
- One coffee maker
- A potato masher thingy
- A whisk
- A colander
- A cast iron skillet (for biscuits and corn bread)
- Two hot pads and one oven mitt (at least)
- Kitchen towels (four to six)
- At least two dish clothes
- Two sponges
- A kitchen sized trash can
- A meat thermometer and a regular cooking thermometer
- Pizza slicer
- Plastic cutting board
- A pair of scissors

There is not much more that you could need. As you grow in the kitchen, you'll discover more tools and gadgets that can be helpful. For now, however, let's keep in simple.

THE STAPLES

I have several things that I will not run out of in the kitchen. You may have several more things to add. I like to call these "the staples".

Mostly, I keep these things around the kitchen because I use them in a lot of different recipes or because they are the main ingredient in some of those recipes. Nonetheless, they are always at the top of my grocery list.

I have a preference of brand for some of the items and, as you grow in the kitchen, you may find your own preference.

- Margarine (or butter)
- Self-rising flour
- Self rising corn meal
- Coffee
- Eggs
- Cheese
- Ketchup
- Mustard
- Mayonnaise
- Milk
- Fruit Juice (fresh, frozen or canned)
- Cooking oil
- Cooking spray
- Salt
- Pepper
- Garlic powder
- Italian seasoning
- Poultry seasoning
- Potatoes
- Onions
- Dry cereal
- Grits (yes, I am a southern boy)
- Loaf bread
- Hot sauce
- Paper towels
- Soft scrub cleaner (never use harsh cleaners on a glass cook top)
- Dishwashing detergent
- SOS scrubbing pads or equivalent
- Clorox spray cleaner or equivalent
- Kitchen sized trash bags
- Sandwich bags (for leftovers)
- Quart sized freezer bags (for leftovers)

Again, these are just the basics. As you choose your recipes for the week, you'll find that you need to buy the meats or the vegetables.

Your list of basics will grow as you learn.

A Trip to the Market

When buying fresh produce, look for any brown spots. Brown spots normally mean the product is bruised or old. Try to choose from the bottom. The store clerks put the freshest produce on the bottom because people normally pick from the top.

When choosing meats, look at the date. Also, look at the price-per-pound. A t-bone steak that weighs eight ounces will always be cheaper than a rib-eye that weighs two pounds. But, if you look at the price-per-pound, you realize what you are getting.

The same goes for chicken: Chicken breasts, which have more meat, will cost more, per pound, than chicken legs. But, the legs have brown meat and the breasts have white meat. I wouldn't really recommend doing what Mama used to do. She used to buy the whole chicken and cut it up at home. But, if you are an adventurist (or have a good life insurance), go for it.

When buying fish and seafood, stick to what you know. Just because the "Blue Grungy" is on sale this week for 99 cents per pound, it doesn't mean that your family needs to eat it. If you have never seen it on a restaurant's menu anywhere, don't buy it.

If bread or baked goods are on your list, pay attention to the date. No one wants to eat green bread. But, there are times when buying outdated baked goods are not too bad. For instance, if you shop at a grocery store that has its own bakery, check their clearance rack. Often, they'll have a dozen donuts or a cake that just went out of date and they mark it down drastically. If it has sugar in it, it doesn't last but a few days at my house anyway.

Also, it never hurts to check the ads in the newspaper. Don't just look at one ad, look at two or three. Compare brands and sizes. Make notes if you have to. But remember, the grocers put these products into the newspaper ads because they want you to buy them. You don't have to buy what they tell you to buy.

On that note, let's quickly cover coupons. This is a great way to save money but it's also a great way for manufactures to make money as well. What do I mean?

For instance, you see a coupon in the Sunday paper for name-brand mustard for twenty-cents off. Wow! But, wait, the generic brand that you normally buy is already forty-two cents cheaper and is 2 ounces heavier. So, even if you shop at a grocery store that doubles coupon values, it's still cheaper to stick with what you have been buying.

Why do manufacturers print these coupons? To get you to buy their product, of course. Trust me; they don't go through all of the trouble just to help you save money. Just because you use a coupon, it doesn't mean you'll save money. It just means that you will spend money on their product.

And don't forget to make friends with the cashier. You can ask him or her about a certain product. They'll tell you if they sell a lot of it. They may even recommend a cheaper brand.

Lastly, pay in cash. It's something that Dave Ramsey recommends. Studies have shown that you are more careful with cash spending than plastic. If you have a hundred dollar budget, it's a lot easier to go over if you have a card to swipe. But, if you have one hundred dollars in cash, you'll find yourself calculating your total as you fill your buggy.

In the long run, the idea is to make shopping less of a chore. Try making it fun.

When my oldest kids were five and three, we lived in a small town in Virginia. We shopped at the same store every week and even went to the same cashier. I kind of thought that cashier was cute and my baby boy did too, obviously. He would stand there with an open mouth gawking (I probably did too) while she rang up our total. One day, as he drooled, he accidentally belched. Needless to say, we all three left the store a little red-faced. But we laughed about it all the way home.

General Measurements, Abbreviations and Meanings

I am not a rocket scientist but I do live near NASA in Huntsville, Alabama. I don't know the metric system and I never could keep up with how many quarts are in a gallon. Don't ask me how many teaspoons make up a tablespoon and don't even think of asking to borrow a cup of sugar.

Very few people have measurements memorized. Early on, I found a recipe book with a massive amount of measurements printed inside. I never tried any of the recipes in the book but I consulted the measurement table almost weekly for one thing or the other. It helped during a time before the internet.

My advice to you is to print out or copy the measurement table I have included below. Tape it to the back of the cabinet door where you keep the spices and thank me every time you add the right amount of salt or sugar.

Measurements:

A dash=less than 1/8 teaspoon

3 teaspoons = 1 tablespoon

4 tablespoons=1/4 cup

8 tablespoons =1/2 cup

16 tablespoons=1 cup

2 tablespoons of liquid=1 ounce of liquid

1 cup of liquid=8 fluid ounces

2 cups=1 pint

4 cups=1 quart

4 quarts=1 gallon

4 pecks=1 bushel

16 ounces =1 pound

4 quarters = 1 dollar

Abbreviations:

c. is cup

pt. is pint

qt. is quart

pk. Is peck

bu. Is bushel

oz. is ounces

lb. is pound

is pound

Sq. is square

Tsp is teaspoon

Tbsp is tablespoon

Meanings:

Ala mode: This is one of my favorite terms. It means that there is ice cream on it, in it or beside it.

Bake: Cook food in an oven using dry heat.

Baste: Spoon pan liquid (juices) over meats while they are roasting to keep the surface from drying out.

Boil: Cook food in water that has reached a temperature of at least 212 degrees in which bubbles are constantly rising to the surface.

Broil: To cook by direct heat, either under the direct heat of the broiler in the oven, over hot coals on the grill or between two heat sources.

Crepes: Very thin pancakes normally served with fruit and whipped filling.

Fillet: A boneless piece of meat or chicken.

Frothy: this is a term used in a lot of recipes involving eggs. Normally, when you beat an egg briskly, it will get frothy or a milky thickness will develop on top of the eggs which looks a lot like whipped cream except it should have a few bubbles.

Fry: Cook in hot oil or grease.

Grate: To obtain small pieces of a food by rubbing or scraping on a grater or shredder.

Grits: Coarsely ground, dried corn, served boiled.

Marinade: Soak food in seasoned liquid.

Preheat: Turn the oven on to allow the temperature to be reached before the food is placed inside.

Roast: Meat cooked in dry heat in the oven.

Sauté: Fry food quickly over high heat in a small amount of oil or butter.

Sear: To brown the surface of the meat over a high heat, sealing in the juices.

Shred: Pull, cut, slice or tear into stringy, thread like pieces.

Simmer: Cook at a temperature below boiling.

Steam: Cook food with steam using a platform over boiling water.

SAFE FOOD HANDLING

There are monsters in your kitchen. They are in the refrigerator, on the stove, in the sink, in the cupboard, on the floors and even on the counters. These monsters have names like Sal Monella, Bo Tulism, E. Coli and Liz Teria.

Of course, I am making light of something that is very serious. Food-borne illnesses are not a laughing matter. I have had food poisoning. It came from a major restaurant chain while I was out of town on businesses. It was not fun and it still makes my stomach churn every time I look at one of their restaurants or see an advertisement for that chain.

The last thing that you want to happen is for your kids, your wife or your significant other to get some form of food poisoning because of your cooking. Their stomach may churn every time they look at you. Not a good scenario.

You can prevent most food-borne illnesses before they start by following a few simple steps.

- Wash your hands before and after touching any raw meats or eggs. Wash your hands before you prepare vegetables. Wash your hands before you handle bread. Wash your hands before you unload the dishwasher. Wash your hands before you slice cheese. Wash your hands. Wash your hands. Wash your hands. You can really never do this too much. If your hands start drying out, borrow some hand lotion. It's better to be safe and smell like lotion later than to make your whole family sick.
- Rinse fresh vegetables and fruits well, even if they are already in a bag. This even goes for potatoes. There are a lot of bad things on a farm that can contaminate food but there are as many bad things in the processing plant, the trucking terminal and even the store.
- Keep cold things cold. If you bought it from the frozen food section, it needs to be in the freezer at your house. If it was refrigerated in the store, it needs to be refrigerated at your house.
- Cook all meats and eggs well. As a general rule, the interior temperature of your food should be at least 160 degrees before it is removed from the heat. For most poultry products, the recommendation is 165 degrees. The federal and state governments have spent a lot of our money on advertising to make sure we know this. Go to one of their websites and print off a chart to keep in your kitchen.
- Keep raw foods separated. This means that the uncooked ground beef patties shouldn't touch the hamburger bun or even look in that direction until it is cooked.
- Refrigerate leftovers within two hours of cooking.
- Keep all surfaces clean. It's not a bad idea to wipe down the counters and the stove before you cook, while you are cooking and even after you cook. Use a good cleaner that says antibacterial on the label.
- If it has grown hair or has changed color, don't cook it or eat it.

- If it looks ruined or smells rancid, don't use it. Now, this doesn't count as much for sauerkraut, rutabagas and limburger cheese but, even those food items can contain bacteria.
- And finally, if your dog or cat runs from the food, your family should too.

Several years ago, back when my two oldest children were about 12 and 10 years old, I convinced a very good-looking lady to come to my house for dinner. I grilled pork chops, cooked fresh green beans, nuked some potatoes, warmed some nice fresh rolls and made a gallon of that good southern sweet tea.

Once the food was done and we were seated, she asked for sour cream to go on her potato. No problem. We never used sour cream but I distinctively remembered having some in the refrigerator.

With a smile, I excused myself from the table, retrieved the sour cream and a clean spoon and handed her the container. Things were going so well up to this point.

She opened the container. She was not impressed by the fact that the sour cream had grown hair and changed its color to a nice forest green. Oh, and the kids made a big fuss about it too.

I never saw her again. She did stay, at least, until everyone else finished eating but I never saw her again after that. I guess she didn't want to date someone who didn't like sour cream on their potato.

All jokes aside, there are expiration dates on most products. Read them. If I remember correctly, that sour cream had been expired by about fourteen months. I checked it after she left. Check your refrigerator and cupboard often. If it's out of date or spoiled, throw it away.

SETTING MY TABLE

Breakfast growing up was most always a boring thing: one egg, one biscuit and one glass of milk.

It wasn't because Mama thought it was nutritious. She did say, on occasion, that it stuck to your ribs. By the time I was in the ninth grade, biology class dispelled that claim. By my senior year in high school, economics class made me finally realize that this was nothing more than an inexpensive way to feed the five of us boys. Biscuits were cheap when made by hand, an egg apiece was reasonable and the milk just washed down the love and frugality.

There it was, every morning of the week: one egg, a biscuit, a glass of milk and a heaping helping of frugality. The only variation from this would be Saturday morning.

Every Saturday, my mom would make bacon and grits or milk gravy to go along with the egg and biscuit. Quite often, if we were lucky, we would even get two eggs. If we were fast, we would get two biscuits.

Most of the time, what we referred to as bacon was actually fat back or what mama called "strick-o-lean". I never really cared. It was different. It smelled good cooking and I would always be the first of the five kids awake just so I could soak in the smell. It seems a bit trite to most people, but to me, this was a special occasion.

I didn't know that we were poor. I knew we had less than some people but I didn't equate that to being different. The economic part of all of this never came into play until I was older. My real appreciation for these Saturdays wouldn't hit for many years to come.

Back then, we would sit as a family and eat breakfast on Saturday morning. Two of us boys would be at the kitchen table with Mama and Daddy, the other three boys at the bar between the kitchen and dining room.

Mom would always sit sideways to the table. I once asked her why and she seemed puzzled. It was like she, herself, had forgotten why she sat this way. She told us she was more comfortable like that but I figured it was because of all the feet under that old oak table. There just wasn't enough room for her but she never complained.

I learned to enjoy the simple pleasures of life with my feet under that old oak table on Saturday morning. Through the years, we had the same table but many different plates. Five clumsy boys made sure of that. The funny thing is that I can recall the table and I can recall what was on the plate but I can't picture the actual plate. I appreciated it. But I can't recall it.

Most of the time, the fork would fail to match the spoon. Well, maybe they did match because they were both silver in color but the patterns were seldom the same. I came to appreciate this as well because it was something different. Mama always kept one set that all matched in a safe place for company. The funny thing is that I don't really ever remember having company coming over to eat. Maybe it was because there were too many feet under the table.

Breakfast seemed to last a long time back then. We would pray and we would eat. Not much was ever said. No one declared their plans for the day. No one talked about the weather. No one really ever spoke. We just ate. Mama always had an old AM radio playing in the background. Most of the time, it played country music. Sometimes it was the news. We never really paid it much attention. It was just part of the kitchen.

We had a washer and a dryer in the kitchen as well. During meals, it served as a buffet. I never saw anything wrong with a plate full of fluffy white biscuits sitting on that old brown dryer. It was part of the kitchen and the kitchen was where we ate.

There were never any biscuits left on the dryer after breakfast anyway. As a matter of fact, there was never anything left on any of the plates. I would, later in life, come to understand this to be a compliment to the cook.

As the years went by, I never stopped to look at that kitchen as much as I do today. The kitchen was a focal point in our family home. It divided the rest of the house from the den. We walked through it dozens of times each day. We ate there. We drank there. We fussed there. We got our whippings there for fussing or fighting. We grew up in that kitchen. We never really stopped, though, and appreciated what it meant to our family.

I haven't been back in that kitchen since I was 21. It has, no doubt, been remodeled countless times from the pine paneling, green linoleum and single frosted light fixture. It was good enough for us. There wasn't a lot of room but we didn't need a lot. There wasn't a lot a light but we could see just fine anyway. We didn't have a dishwasher. We didn't have an ice maker.

The old oak table was lost it in a move. The spoons and forks, I am confident, gave up on finding their mates. Plates that met an untimely demise probably still haunt the cupboards early on Saturday mornings. And the feet from my youth have all gone away. Mama and Daddy, too.

Breakfast taught me a lot about eggs and feet and thriftiness. Most of all, it taught me about love and traditions.

Years later, as a young man, I found myself to be a single Dad to two wonderful kids. I also found the chance to repeat traditions. Shanna, my first child, and Bryant never saw it coming.

We lived in Georgia then Virginia then back in Georgia and finally to Alabama. We had an octagonal table, a square table and long table. I don't ever recall owning a round table. The tables were all wood but not oak. Well, there were particles of wood, pressed together in a factory. It seemed like wood I guess. They all seemed to have enough room underneath for feet.

We had plates but they never did catch my eye any more than Mama's plates did. I always tried to have matching silverware but often failed.

Despite the years and the obvious differences, Saturday morning became special again, at least to me.

Most mornings during the week, Shanna and Bryant had cold cereal before school. Eggs and a biscuit were available but never called into service. The biscuits stayed in the freezer and the eggs lived a lonely week in the fridge. Yes, I found myself being frugal as a single parent but saving a few minutes was as important to me as saving a few pennies.

But, not on Saturday.

Saturday was when I would cook a big breakfast. I had learned how to make milk gravy like Mama and Aunt Nora used to make. That was a watershed point in my life. Neither my mother nor my aunt was around to test my recipe but I thought it was good. We had grits most of the time but once we moved to Virginia, grits were scarce. I learned the milk gravy recipe almost out of necessity. Bless my babies; it was a trial of errors.

As the years went by, I began to feel giddy on Friday night while planning Saturday morning breakfast.

I learned how to make banana pancakes. I still couldn't make biscuits from scratch but I could knock that can up against the counter with the best cooks. I learned which cheese to use in the grits and how much. I found the lost art of flipping eggs.

I never did learn how to sit sideways at the table although I do remember trying it one time. It seemed extremely uncomfortable for me. Mama always bragged that she never told a lie.

As more years passed, I realized how proud I was to get up and make that Saturday morning breakfast for the kids. I was carrying on a tradition.

I assume Saturday morning breakfast was special for Shanna and Bryant. They never really said it was special. I do have a feeling that one day they will glance back into the old kitchens in Georgia, Virginia and Alabama and see what I see today. I guess that's the thing about traditions: for a tradition to be real, time has to pass. I am sure they'll never embrace it until later anyway.

There we were, anyway, a single Dad and two kids. A table, some plates, mismatched spoons and forks, eggs, milk gravy and frozen biscuits. And love.

Shanna and Bryant grew up. Their feet are now under someone else's table.

Shanna is married, a college graduate and lives in Georgia. There are just four feet under her table for now.

Bryant is in college and is also a soldier. He has many feet under the table no matter where he sits. Most of the time, lately, his feet are in Iraq but soon they will be in back at the University of Tennessee again.

I miss their feet. I miss their smiles. I miss those days.

I have now started a new family. I remarried and Granger was born a month shy of Bryant's High School graduation. Maggie followed fourteen months later and now we have little Laina. My wife, Val, loves my Saturday morning breakfast. She has made sure that the spoons and forks all match.

We have a pine table now. The plates are all different colors by design. I have learned to make biscuits from scratch. I take them out of the oven, stack them on a plate and serve them from the counter. It's part of the kitchen.

I even have a hot plate to make pancakes. I have an ice maker and a dishwasher in my kitchen. The walls are made of gypsum. There is tile on the floor. We have a chandelier over the table with five lights. We have room to move around.

Most mornings, Granger wakes up with the sunrise much as I did when I was a small child. I see so much of me in him. It makes me remember what all I had growing up. It also helps me forget all that I didn't have growing up.

Mama and Daddy were good providers. We never got all that we wanted. They gave us much of what we needed but we were always practical. I never had a dirt bike. I never went to Disney world. Our birthdays all fell within a few weeks of one another so all we received for a present was a home-made cake of our choice cooked in Mama's kitchen and served from the dryer. Christmas wasn't much different.

I had a tradition, though. This tradition, I have found, would mean more to me than a dirt bike or a trip. They don't sell this stuff in the Christmas catalog.

Shanna and her husband Daryl visit often. Bryant is home when he can make it.

I find myself, when all of my children are home, almost overcome as I cook breakfast on Saturday morning. Is it a chore? No, not at all. It's more like a privilege.

I have eggs. I have bacon. I even have home-made biscuits and gravy. I have Fiesta ware plates that don't match by design but my spoons agree with my forks.

I have five kids now just like Mama and Daddy. I also have a table. Under that table I have feet, lots of feet. And under those feet I have a tradition. I wonder if this is how Mama and Daddy felt.

(From a collection of short stories about growing up, by Stan Reese, 2009)

Breakfast

BREAKFAST

Studies have shown that breakfast is the most important meal of the day.

While that may be true, everyone who works a regular job knows that breakfast can also be one of the busiest times of the day.

Not only do we have to roll ourselves out of bed before we hit snooze for the third time but we also have to shower, shave, brush our teeth, comb our hair, get dressed and then think about what to eat. Plus, if you have children, a spouse or a roommate, the stress can become multiplied.

I get tired just thinking about it.

But, breakfast is actually my favorite meal and I have been known to cook breakfast foods for dinner.

On the following pages you will find some very simple recipes for breakfast (or supper) foods. Feel free to add or take away ingredients to fit your taste. Some people may like more pepper, some may like less salt. Don't be afraid. Relax-Dad. It's just the most important meal of the day and you are already fifteen minutes late for work.

SCRAMBLED CHEESY EGGS

Tools needed:
Large stainless steel frying pan
Metal spatula
½ cup measuring cup
Mixing bowl

Ingredients:
5 eggs
¼ cup of milk
1/8 teaspoon of salt
1/8 teaspoon of black pepper
½ cup of shredded cheddar cheese
Cooking spray

   Turn on a large eye on the stove to medium heat. Spray the inside of the stainless steel frying pan. Do not put the pan on the stove yet! Break five eggs individually into a medium sized mixing bowl. Discard the shells. Add ¼ cup of milk, salt and pepper and mix briskly with a fork or whisk until frothy. Pour mixture into the frying pan and place the pan on the heated eye. Do not stir yet. Wait about three minutes before stirring but if you see the eggs start to bubble, it's time to stir them with the spatula. Keep the eggs turned with the spatula, actually scrambling them gently. Once they start to look dry, remove the pan from heat and sprinkle with the cheese. Allow the cheese to melt and serve warm with biscuits, toast or muffins.

Feeds: 3

Notes:

FRIED EGGS

At this point, let me explain how easy it is to make green eggs and ham. All you have to do is add a drop or two of green food coloring to an egg before cooking. It's impressive and you would think that any child would be tickled to eat the infamous green eggs. But, nooooo. I have tried it twice. The eggs taste the same but there is just something about green eggs that makes it less palatable. Don't try it at home. Leave this to the fairy tale books.

Tools needed:
Large frying pan
Metal spatula
Small glass

Ingredients:
5 eggs
Salt
Pepper
Cooking spray

Generously coat the stainless steel frying pan with cooking spray. If you would rather use butter, this is okay but I prefer spray. Place the pan on the large eye of the stove on medium heat. If you are using butter, let the butter melt first. Crack open the eggs into a small glass one at a time. This will allow you to fish out any egg shells before they go into the pan. Discard the eggs shells and put the cracked egg on the pan one at a time. Add just a dash of salt and pepper to each egg. Once the egg whites actually start looking white, reduce the heat to medium low to prevent burning. Once the egg whites are white all the way to the yellow, carefully push the spatula under the egg and, in a controlled motion, flip the egg over so that the other side cooks. This is what is referred to "over easy". Allow the egg to cook a few more minutes. Remove the pan from the eye and take up the eggs with the spatula. Serve warm with biscuits or toast.

Feeds: 3

Notes:

BAKED EGGS AND CANADIAN BACON

This recipe sounds fancy and hard but it's really fancy and easy. And, since it's baked, it's not too bad for you either.

Tools needed:
Muffin pan
Small plastic spatula
½ cup measuring cup
Medium mixing bowl

Ingredients:
5 eggs
5 pieces of Canadian bacon
Salt
pepper
¼ cup of milk
½ cup of shredded mozzarella cheese

Preheat oven to 325 degrees. Generously coat the inside of a muffin pan with cooking spray. Crack open five eggs into a medium mixing bowl, discarding the shells. Add ¼ cup milk, 1/8 teaspoon salt and 1/8 teaspoon of pepper. You can add a touch of Italian seasoning for taste if you would like. Beat the eggs, milk and spices briskly with a fork or whisk until frothy. Now, add one piece of Canadian bacon to the bottom of six muffin ports in the muffin pan. Pour in the egg mixture so that the same amount goes in each port. Top with mozzarella cheese and place into the oven. Cook for thirty minutes in the oven or until the eggs begin to brown. Clean up your mess while the eggs cook. After thirty minutes, remove the pan from the oven with a hot pad and use the small plastic spatula to remove the eggs from the pan. Serve warm with muffins or fruit.

Feeds: 3

Notes:

BREAKFAST CASSEROLE

This recipe is one of my wife favorites. I normally "allow" her to cook this just so that she will feel useful around the kitchen. It's nice to have someone else cook every now and again. Remember that, guys. The recipe below uses sausage but you could substitute that for bacon or ham.

Tools needed:
Small frying pan
Eight inch pie pan (glass or metal)
Medium mixing bowl
½ cup measuring cup

Ingredients:
5 eggs
½ pound of sausage
¼ cup of milk
½ cup of grated cheddar cheese
1 frozen pie crust
Salt
Pepper
Italian seasoning
1/8 cup of finely chopped onions or scallions

Preheat the oven to 350 degrees. Cook the sausage over a medium heat, using a fork to stir and tear the sausage so that is cooks loosely like taco meat. Generously spray the inside of an eight inch pie plate. Take the frozen pie crust and unwrap it gently into the pie plate. Place the pie crust into the oven for a few minutes while you work on the egg mixture (this allows the crust to spread out and begin to cook).

In a mixing bowl, crack open five eggs, discarding the shells. Add ¼ cup of milk, 1/8 teaspoon of salt, 1/8 teaspoon of pepper, a dash of Italian seasoning, ½ cup of cheese, ½ pound of cooked sausage and 1/8 cup of finely chopped onion. Mix these ingredients together well using a fork. Remove the pie plate and crust from the oven with hot pads and carefully readjust the crust. It may have sagged down in some areas because it was unthawing. That's perfectly fine, just use the tips of your fingers to gently pull it back into place and allow it to hang over the edge slightly. Now, pour in the egg mixture and place the pie plate back into the oven. Cook for about 35 minutes or until the top looks slightly brown. Clean up your mess while it's cooking. Remove from the oven with hot pads and slice it like you would pie. Serve warm with muffins or fruit and be prepared to receive accolades.

Feeds: 3

Notes:

BISCUITS

My Mamma, rest her soul, made the best biscuits in the world. She used to talk about how, at the age of five, her own mother had died and her Granny taught her how to make biscuits. Mamma said she used to push a chair up to the counter and make biscuits until she was old enough to reach everything herself.

I didn't even try to make my first biscuit until I was 28. It was not pretty and it didn't taste very well either. It could have made a better weapon. I never gave up, though and several years later, they finally started coming out edible. I guess practice does make perfect.

Tools needed:
Large cast iron skillet
Medium mixing bowl
Fork

Ingredients:
2 cups of self-rising flour
1 cup of buttermilk
5 table spoons of margarine

Preheat the oven to 390 degrees. If you are using a cast iron skillet that has been cured, there is no need to spray it with cooking spray. But, if it's not cured, you can rub it with shortening. If you are using a cake pan or pie plate, spray the inside with an even coat of cooking spray. In a medium mixing bowl, pour in the two cups of flour. I never sift mine but you can. Add five tablespoons of margarine and one cup of buttermilk. Begin mixing with your fork but, honestly, the best results will be obtained by using your hands. Mix it all up real good and separate out into pieces about the size of a golf ball, placing them into the iron skillet which, hopefully, has been cured. Put the skillet in the oven and clean up your mess while it cooks. Serve with butter and jelly or jam but my favorite is to serve it with milk gravy.

Makes about 6 or 7 biscuits, depending on the size of the biscuit.

Feeds: 3-4

Notes:

MILK GRAVY

There is a reason why this recipe follows, directly, the recipe for biscuits. If you have never had a good biscuit smothered with good milk gravy (or white gravy), you haven't really eaten breakfast. And, since it is the most important meal of the day, this is the back bone of a good breakfast.

Now, don't panic if your gravy is lumpy or too thick or too thin. Gravy is good. Say it. Gravy is good.

Tools needed:
Small sauce pan
Wooden (preferably) spoon

Ingredients:
7 tablespoons of butter (drippings from cooking bacon or sausage can also be used)
7 tablespoons of self rising flour
A dash of salt
A dash of pepper
2 cups of milk

Turn on the small eye on the stove to just past half way. Melt the butter. As soon as the butter is melted, remove the pan from the eye and slowly add the flour, salt and pepper, mixing together to a thin past. Add ¼ cup of milk, mixing until that is pasty. Return the pan to the eye, stirring often. Once the mixture starts to become thick, add another ½ cup until all of the milk has been used. Be careful not to let the mixture boil or scorch. Once all of the milk has been used, continue to stir until the gravy thickens. Remove from heat and serve.

Feeds: 3-5 depending on what part of the country they are from.

Notes:

BANANA PANCAKES

I discovered this recipe purely by chance and necessity. I was living in Virginia with my two small kids. Syrup was on sale and so was bananas. Since they liked pancakes, I decided to see what I could do with the bananas. They are grown now but Shanna and Bryant still like my banana pancakes as does my wife's cousin. Someone even wrote a song about it but I am sure it wasn't about my own recipe.

Tools needed:
A blender
A plastic spatula
An electric skillet
Butter knife
¼ cup measuring cup
1 cup measuring cup

Ingredients:
2 cups of buttermilk
1 egg
¼ cup of vegetable oil
2 cups of self rising flour
1 teaspoon of vanilla extract

Plug in the skillet and turn the temperature up to 350 degrees or about ¾ of the way to high. In a blender, combine the buttermilk, egg, vegetable oil and vanilla flavoring. Add the flour ½ cup at a time and continue to blend until smooth. The consistency of the batter should be like a milk shake. If it's too thin, add a little flour. If it's too thick, add a little milk. Now, thinly slice two bananas lengthwise and leave to the side.

Pour the batter, ¼ cup at a time, onto the electric skillet. Carefully add two slices of the banana to each pancake, allowing it to sink down slightly into the batter. Lift the edges after 2-3 minutes to see if the bottom has browned. Once brown on the bottom, flip the pancake. Don't get too fancy, just turn it over.

Allow the other side to brown and then remove the pancake, adding butter to the top. Serve with syrup or honey.

Feeds: about 3-5

Notes:

RAISIN PANCAKES

This is probably the first recipe I ever successfully tried. As I remember, I was attempting to impress someone. I don't remember if it worked but the recipe has stuck with me ever since. So, yeah, it probably did work.

Tools needed:
A blender
A plastic spatula
An electric skillet
Butter knife
¼ cup measuring cup
1 cup measuring cup

Ingredients:
2 cups of buttermilk (or regular milk)
2 eggs
½ cup of raisins
¼ cup of dates (optional)
¼ cup of vegetable oil
2 cups of self rising flour

Plug in the skillet and turn the temperature up to 350 degrees or about ¾ of the way to high. In a blender, combine the buttermilk, egg and vegetable oil. Add the flour ½ cup at a time and continue to blend until smooth. The consistency of the batter should be like a milk shake. If it's too thin, add a little flour. If it's too thick, add a little milk. Once the proper consistency has been reached, add the raisins and the optional dates. Blend for no more than 5-10 seconds. You don't want to shred the raisins; you only want to blend them into the batter.

Pour the batter, ¼ cup at a time, onto the electric skillet. Lift the edges after 2-3 minutes to see if the bottom has browned. Once the bottom is brown, flip the pancake. Don't get too fancy, just turn it over.

Allow the other side to brown and then remove the pancake, adding butter to the top. Serve with syrup or honey.

Feeds: about 3-5

Notes:

APPLE CINA-MAN PANCAKES

This is my wife's favorite. Subsequently, it has become a favorite for my three babies as well. Now, when I cook pancakes, I have to cook three different types. A man's work is never done.

Tools needed:
A blender
A plastic spatula
An electric skillet
Butter knife
Paring knife
¼ cup measuring cup
1 cup measuring cup

Ingredients:
2 cups of buttermilk (or regular milk)
1 egg
1 apple
1/8 teaspoon of cinnamon
1 teaspoon of vanilla extract
¼ cup of brown sugar
¼ cup of vegetable oil
2 cups of self rising flour

Plug in the skillet and turn the temperature up to 350 degrees or about ¾ of the way to high. In a blender, combine the buttermilk, egg, vegetable oil and vanilla flavoring. Add the flour ½ cup at a time and continue to blend until smooth. The consistency of the batter should be like a milk shake. If it's too thin, add a little flour. If it's too thick, add a little milk.

Peel an apple and slice pieces off of the apple thinly. Lay the slices to the side.

Pour the batter, ¼ cup at a time, onto the electric skillet. Add slices of apple, allowing them to settle into the battle. Sprinkle lightly with cinnamon. Lift the edges after 2-3 minutes to see if the bottom has browned. Once the bottom is brown, flip the pancake. Don't get too fancy, just turn it over.

Allow the other side to brown and then remove the pancake, adding butter to the top. Serve with syrup or honey.

Feeds: about 3-5

Notes:

CHOCOLATE CHIP PANCAKES

I love chocolate and I love pancakes. This combines the best of both worlds.

Tools needed:
A blender
A plastic spatula
An electric skillet
Butter knife
¼ cup measuring cup
1 cup measuring cup

Ingredients:
2 cups of buttermilk (or regular milk)
2 eggs
¼ cup of vegetable oil
½ cup of chocolate chips (butterscotch ships can be substituted)
2 cups of self rising flour

Plug in the skillet and turn the temperature up to 350 degrees or about ¾ of the way to high. In a blender, combine the buttermilk, egg and vegetable oil. Add the flour ½ cup at a time and continue to blend until smooth. The consistency of the batter should be like a milk shake. If it's too thin, add a little flour. If it's too thick, add a little milk. Once the proper consistency has been reached, add the chocolate chips. Blend for no more than 5-10 seconds. You don't want to break up the chocolate chips; you only want to blend them into the batter.

Pour the batter, ¼ cup at a time, onto the electric skillet. Lift the edges after 2-3 minutes to see if the bottom has browned. Once the bottom is brown, flip the pancake. Don't get too fancy, just turn it over.

Allow the other side to brown and then remove the pancake, adding butter to the top. Serve with syrup or honey.

Feeds: about 3-5

Notes:

CHEESY GRITS

If you are not from the southern part of the United States, you probably don't know about the joy of grits. Instead, you probably ask yourself "what is a grit?". Well, one dictionary I looked in didn't even have grits in it. The next dictionary identified grits as a finely ground corn food of the American Indian. I didn't know that. I did know that grits are good and they get better with cheese.

By the way, you can buy instant grits in packets but they are not as good as the "old fashioned grits" you can buy at most southern stores.

Tools needed:
Medium sauce pan
Medium frying pan
Spatula
1 cup measuring cup
Large spoon

Ingredients:
1 cup of quick grits (not instant)
2 cups of water
½ cup of shredded cheddar cheese
3 tablespoons of butter
3 eggs
Salt and pepper to taste

Add two cups of water and 1/8 teaspoon salt to a medium sauce pan. Place the pan on the stove and turn the eye on to high. Once the water begins to boil, slowly add one cup of grits and turn the eye down to medium low. Stir the grits often as they cook. Once the grits begin to thicken, turn the eye down to low. Add three tablespoons of butter and ½ cup of shredded cheese. Stir and allow the cheese and butter to melt.

Turn another eye on the stove on to half way to high. Spray the inside of the frying pan generously with cooking spray and place onto the eye. Crack three eggs open into a glass. Do not break the yokes (the yellows). Gently pour the eggs into the frying pan cooking until the clear part becomes white. Turn the eggs over gently and cook the other side until the white just outside of the yoke is solid.

On a large plate, add two large spoons full of grits and one egg. Stir the two together on the plate and serve with biscuits or toast.

Feeds: 3

Notes:

MUFFINS

Muffins are a very simple recipe to make for breakfast. You can buy the muffin mix at the store and follow the directions or, with a stocked cupboard, you can easily make them from scratch. The greatest thing about cooking muffins from scratch is that you can add extra ingredients and call it your own. I like blueberries or dates. You can try raisins, cranberries, strawberries, walnuts or anything else that might sound good.

Tools needed:
Muffin pan
Medium mixing bowl
A large fork or a whisk
A large spoon
¼ cup measuring cup
2 cup measuring cup
Teaspoon

Ingredients:
2 cups of self rising flour
1 cup of milk
¼ cup of sugar
1 egg
1/8 cup of vegetable oil
½ cup of berries and/or nuts

Turn the oven on to 400 degrees. Generously coat the inside of a muffin pan or add the paper cupcake cups that you can buy at the store. In a medium or large mixing bowl, combine the milk, eggs, vegetable oil and sugar. Stir vigorously until well mixed. Add the flour, one cup at a time until well mixed. Add the berries or nuts. Once the ingredients are the consistency of a milk shake, spoon it into the ports of the muffin pan. They ports should not be filled more than ¾ of the way to the top because the muffins will rise when they are baked.

Place the pan into the pre-heated oven for about 20 minutes. You can check to make sure they are done by placing a tooth pick or butter knife through the top of one of the muffins. If it comes out clean, they are done. If there is batter on the tooth pick or knife, they aren't quite ready yet.

Feeds: 3-5

Notes:

LUNCH

LUNCH

Lunch, by nature, is a very simple meal. There are as many sandwiches and sandwich combinations out there as there are people. Every person likes things differently and this is especially true of sandwiches.

My youngest son loves bologna and cheese with mayonnaise. Sure, it's not the healthiest lunch in the world but he eats this better than he would a Rueben sandwich. In the long run, the fact that he actually eats is what matters.

My two youngest daughters love peanut butter and jelly. One likes her sandwich cut into four squares while the other prefers four triangles. Not only is peanut butter a healthy food but it has also helped them learn their shapes.

Myself, I prefer tuna salad and my mother-in-law makes the best tuna salad. I try but I can never seem to recreate her recipe. She says it's nothing special but it is. The whole thing with cooking is to make it special (but keep it simple).

I didn't put too many lunch recipes in this book. I think I'll do a whole book of lunch recipes later on. For now, let's focus on the basics.

BOILED WATER

I know, this is the simplest recipe in the whole book but a lot of guys don't even know how to boil water. I didn't know how to boil water when I suddenly became a single Dad in 1989. It really all starts here because you boil water for a lot of recipes.

Tools needed:
Medium saucepan

Ingredients:
Water

Add four cups of regular tap water to a medium saucepan. Place the pan on a large eye on the stove. Turn the eye on to high. Do not watch the pot. This is important. A watched pot never boils, according to old sayings. I've never actually stood there and tried. Let me know if it works for you.

Once the steam starts coming out of the water and bubbles continuously rise from the bottom, this is an indication that the water has reached the proper temperature to be considered boiling. Make sure you remove the pot from the eye before all the water is evaporated. This could start a fire if the dry pot continues to get hot. It may eventually melt the metal or the handle. Turn the stove off. Congratulations, you have just boiled water. Don't let anyone ever take that away from you.

HOT DOGS

It's the all-American food and it was an every-other day food at my house in 1989. It's easy to cook and kids love it. As a matter of fact, my oldest son once wrote a poem about hotdogs. He was seven but he was not afraid to profess his love for hot dogs.

Tools needed:
Medium saucepan
Tongs

Ingredients:
Wieners (I prefer all meat wieners but you can get beef, pork, chicken or even turkey franks)
Weiner buns
Ketchup
Mustard

In a medium saucepan, boil four cups of water. Add wieners. Cook on high for about five minutes. Remove from heat. Using tongs, remove individual wieners from the pan, allowing each to drip dry before placing each wiener into a bun. Add ketchup and mustard to taste.

You can also add onions, shredded cheese, chili, pickles, relish, sauerkraut, slaw or even jalapeno peppers. That's the best thing about hot dogs, the possibilities are endless. My favorite is ketchup and mustard with onions and chili. I also like ketchup, mustard and slaw. My wife likes sauerkraut. I have never met a hot dog I didn't like.

Serve with macaroni and cheese, potato salad or chips.

Feeds: 3-4

TUNA SALAD

Tools needed:
Medium saucepan
Medium mixing bowl
Fork
2 table spoons
1 teaspoon
Knife

Ingredients:
2 eggs
1 can of tuna in water
1 tablespoon of mayonnaise
1 tablespoon of sweet pickle relish
1 teaspoon of mustard
1 teaspoon of dehydrated onions
6 slices of bread
Salt and pepper to taste

In a medium saucepan, add four cups of water and two eggs with just a dash of salt to help prevent cracking of the egg shells while boiling. Turn on the eye to high and allow the water to begin boiling. Let the eggs cook on high for five minutes. Remove the pan from the stove, pour off the hot water and run cold water over the eggs for about forty-five seconds.

While the eggs cook in the water, open the can of tuna and put it into a medium mixing bowl. Add one tablespoon of mayonnaise, one teaspoon of mustard, one tablespoon of sweet pickle relish and a teaspoon of dehydrated onions. Mix the ingredients well.

Peel the eggs, discarding the shells. Rinse the eggs to make sure all shells are removed. Chop the eggs up finely and add them to the tuna mixture, mixing well. Place a cover or paper towel over the bowl and allow the tuna salad to chill in the refrigerator for five to ten minutes.

Toast the bread in the toaster. With a spoon, spread the tuna salad across one piece of toast, add salt and pepper to taste and top it with another piece of toast. You can also add a few leaves of lettuce and even tomato or you can leave off the toast all together and serve it directly on lettuce with a side of tomatoes.

Feeds: 3

Notes:

GRILLED HAM AND CHEESE SANDWICH

Grilled ham and cheese is probably one of the easiest warm lunches to cook. But, when you add a secret ingredient, it just makes it better.

Tools needed:
Electric skillet
Plastic spatula
Butter knife

Ingredients:
6 slices of ham luncheon meat (doesn't have to be fancy)
6 slices of bread (I like to use whole wheat)
3 slices of cheddar cheese
Butter
Italian seasoning

Turn the electric skillet on to 350 degrees or to about ¾ of the way to high. Butter one side of the six slices of bread and place them on the skillet. Add two slices of ham and one slice of cheese to three of the slices of bread and top with just a dash of Italian seasoning. Place the other three slices of bread, butter side up, on top of the cheese. Grill until the bottom slice is toasted and flip over to allow the top side to toast. Slice into triangles and squares and serve hot with soup or chips.

Feeds: 3

Notes:

THE AUBIE DANG

This is simply a grilled bologna and cheese sandwich. I call it an Aubie Dang because it's really full of bologna and cheese.

Tools needed:
Electric skillet
Plastic spatula
Butter knife

Ingredients:
6 slices of bread
3 thick slices of bologna
3 slices of American cheese

Turn the electric skilled on to 350 degrees or about ¾ of the way to high. Place the bologna on the skillet and slice part of the way but not all of the way to the center in four directions. This will allow the bologna to heat up without curling around the edges.

Butter one side of the six slices of bread while the bologna is heating up. Once the bologna has started to turn slightly brown, use the spatula to take up the bologna and add the bologna to the unbuttered side of three slices of the bread. Place those three slices of bread, butter-side down, onto the skillet and place a slice of cheese on top of the bologna. Now place the other three slices of bread, butter-side up, on top of the cheese. Once the bottom slice has toasted, flip the sandwich over and allow the top slice to toast. Slice into triangles or squares and serve warm with soup or chips.

Feeds: 3

Notes:

BURGER BURGER

I don't cook this often but when I do, it is twice as good as any other burger. Thus, the name: Burger Burger. If cholesterol is a concern, I'd only do this once every now and again.

Tools needed:
Frying pan
Spatula
Knife

Ingredients:
1 pound of lean ground beef
5 slices of bacon
3 medium mushrooms
1 small onion
3 slices of cheddar cheese
3 hamburger buns
Ketchup
Mustard

Turn the eye on the stove to about ¾ of the way to high. Cut the five slices of bacon in half and place into the frying pan. Cook the bacon until slightly crisp, turning to cook both sides. Remove the bacon and set to the side. Turn off the stove and remove the pan from the hot eye temporarily.

Wash the mushrooms and slice them, length-wise into pieces about 1/8 inch think. Place the mushrooms into the warm pan. Turn the eye back to about half way to high and quickly cook both sides. This shouldn't take but 2-3 minutes. Once this is complete, remove the pan from the heat again temporarily. Set the mushrooms aside with the bacon.

Shape the ground beef into three equal size patties and place into the pan. Wash your hands now because raw meat contains bacteria. Cook the ground beef well on both sides. You can use a knife to gently slice into the patty to make sure the inside is brown and not still red.

While the patties are cooking, slice an onion with a clean knife into pieces about 1/8 inch thick. Add ketchup and mustard as desired to the buns. Top the bottom bun with onions and mushrooms followed by one slice of cheese and three slices of bacon. Once the patties are cooked thoroughly, add the patties on top of the cheese and enjoy.

Feeds: at least 3

Notes:

OAKIE SANDWICH

I kind of named this sandwich after the town we lived in several years ago. At times, we didn't have much money and sandwiches were always easy. By this time, it was just me and my oldest son: two men and our appetites. I had not met my current wife and three babies weren't even dreamed of. Times were simple then, just me and Bryant.

Tools needed:
Butter knife

Ingredients:
Bread (preferably hoagie rolls, slice in two pieces)
Meat (ham, turkey, bologna, liverwurst or anything else you like)
Lettuce
Cheese
Mayonnaise and mustard

Slice a hoagie in two (or, if you are just using regular loaf bread, take out two pieces of bread), add mayonnaise to one slice and mustard to the other. Place the two pieces, condiment side up, on a plate. Add one piece of meat then one piece of cheese then one piece of meat and a leaf of lettuce. Repeat these steps as many times as you would like until you get the size sandwich that you like. Serve with potato salad, pasta or chips.

Feeds: 1 or 2

Notes:

CHEESE QUESADILLA

I really like Tex-Mex food but my babies don't. So, whenever I have burritos, I just make these for the kids. It's very simple and satisfying.

Tools needed:
Large frying pan
Spatula
Pizza slicer

Ingredients:
4 large flour tortillas
Cooking spray
1 cup of Shredded Mexican style cheese

Turn the eye for the stove to about half way to high. Spray the inside of the frying pan with cooking spray. Place one tortilla into the pan; place the pan onto the eye. Add about ½ cup of shredded cheese and cover with the other tortilla shell. Pull up the edges often. Once the bottom tortilla starts toasting, flip the quesadilla to the other side. Once that side is done, remove to a plate and slice into sections using a pizza slicer.

Feeds: 3 kids

Notes:

HOGS IN A QUILT

This recipe has been around for years as a party food called pigs in a blanket. I like using the large hot dog wieners and cooking them much like you would a corn dog. Most recipes call for canned biscuits but I prefer using homemade biscuit dough which you will find in the breakfast recipes. Both ways, it's an easy recipe and it's a nice alternative to regular hotdogs.

Tools needed:
Cutting board
Cookie sheet

Ingredients:
Biscuit dough (found in the breakfast section)
Six wieners
Cooking spray

Preheat the oven to 390 degrees. Follow the directions in the breakfast section and make the biscuit dough (or open the can biscuits). Gently sprinkle a large cutting board with flour and roll the dough out onto the cutting board surface. Using a drinking glass, roll the dough and spread it to about 1/8 inch thick. Cut the dough into a sheet almost the length of a wiener. Now, starting from one side, roll one wiener until it's completely covered by the dough. Do not overlap the dough. Cut the dough and press the two sides together. Place onto the cookie sheet with the connection side facing down. Bake at 390 degrees for twenty minutes. Remove from the oven after twenty minutes using an oven mitt or hot pad. Serve warm with ketchup and mustard.

Feeds: 3

Notes:

DINNER

(aka Supper)

DINNER (ALSO KNOWN AS SUPPER)

Dinner, or as some refer to it, supper, is the one meal of the day when families are supposed to sit around the table and share.

At our table now, we each share our favorite part of the day. With three small kids under the age of six, this is sometimes an adventure. But, it's nothing compared to growing up with mom and dad and five sons around the table. That was a quest.

Whether your table has two chairs or twelve, the best part of cooking dinner is being a family.

BEEF ROAST WITH POTATOES AND CARROTS

This is a very simple recipe made in a crock pot. You can start the crock pot in the morning and serve the meal hot after work. The hardest part is waiting.

Tools needed:
Crockpot
Can opener

Ingredients:
3 pound beef pot roast
2 cans of white or "new" potatoes
2 cans of carrots
2 tablespoons of soy sauce
1 teaspoon of Italian seasoning
1 teaspoon of pepper
1 cup of water

Place the beef roast in the crock pot and drizzle with soy sauce. Add the potatoes then the carrots, Sprinkle with the Italian seasoning and pepper. Add enough water to make sure that the roast is covered, normally around one cup. Set the heat on low and cover. In about eight hours, you will have a roast that will be so tender that you won't need a knife. Serve with rolls.

Feeds: 3-4

Notes:

POTATO SALAD

Tools needed:
Large pot
Small pot
Serving bowl
Large fork
Teaspoon
Tablespoon
Potato peeler

Ingredients:
5 or 6 medium potatoes
2 eggs
2 tablespoons of sweet pickle relish
1 tablespoon of mayonnaise
1 teaspoon of mustard
Salt and pepper to taste

    Add four cups of water to the large pot and two cups of water to the small pot, placing both on the stove, with the eyes on high. Peel the potatoes and then cut them into pieces no larger than a golf ball. Slowly add the eggs to the small pot and the potatoes to the large pot. Boil the eggs for five minutes, removing the pot from the stove and rinsing the eggs in cold water for about a minute. Peel the eggs and place them into the serving bowl. Use the fork and break up the eggs until they are in small pieces. Add mayonnaise, mustard and pickle relish.

    Once the potatoes have boiled for about twelve minutes, remove from heat and rinse on cold water. Drain. Add the potatoes to the egg mixture and mix. The potatoes should fall apart on their own. Do not mash like creamed potatoes. They should remain somewhat chunky. Mix well. Add salt and pepper to taste. You can also add more mayonnaise or pickle relish if needed. Serve warm or cold.

Feeds: 3-4

Notes:

CHEESY MASHED POTATOES

Tools needed:
One large pot
1 large fork or a potato masher
Potato peeler
½ cup measuring cup
1 tablespoon
1 teaspoon

Ingredients:
5 for 6 medium potatoes
½ cup of milk
½ cup of shredded cheese
2 tablespoons of butter
½ teaspoon of salt

    Add four cups of water to a large pot and place it on the stove, turning the eye on high. Peel the potatoes and cut into pieces no larger than a golf ball. Slowly add the potatoes to the water. Allow the potatoes to boil for about fifteen minutes. Remove the potatoes from the stove, draining off the excess water by using a colander. Add 2 tablespoons butter, mashing the potatoes as the butter melts. Add ½ cup milk, creaming the potatoes until they are smooth. Add about ½ teaspoon of salt, stirring well. Lastly, add the cheese, stirring until mixed. Serve warm.

Feeds: 3-4

Notes:

GARLIC MASHED POTATOES

Tools needed:
One large pot
Potato peeler
1 large fork or a potato masher
½ cup measuring cup
1 tablespoon
1 teaspoon

Ingredients:
5 for 6 medium potatoes
½ cup of milk
2 tablespoons of butter
½ teaspoon of salt
½ teaspoon of garlic powder

Add four cups of water to a large pot and place it on the stove, turning the eye on high. Peel the potatoes and cut into pieces no larger than a golf ball. Slowly add the potatoes to the water. Allow the potatoes to boil for about fifteen minutes. Remove the potatoes from the stove, draining off the excess water by using a colander. Add 2 tablespoons butter, mashing the potatoes as the butter melts. Add ½ cup milk, creaming the potatoes until they are smooth. Add the salt and the garlic powder, stirring well. More salt or garlic can be added for taste.

Feeds: 3-4

Notes:

POTATO CAKES

There were seldom any leftovers at my house growing up but my mom never wasted anything. That is where this recipe came from: leftovers. You can use the recipe with cheesy mashed potatoes or garlic mashed potatoes or just use plain mashed potatoes. Either way, these things are really good and simple.

Tools needed:
Medium or large frying pan
Medium mixing bowl
¼ cup measuring cup
1 cup measuring cup
1 teaspoon
Small spatula

Ingredients:
About 2 cups of mashed potatoes
1 small onion diced into very small pieces (dehydrated onions would be ok)
1 egg
¼ cup of self rising flour
2 tablespoons of vegetable cooking oil

Add about 2 tablespoons of cooking oil to a frying pan. Place the pan on the stove with the eye just past medium. In a large mixing bowl, add all ingredients, mixing well, Scoop the mixture, one teaspoon at a time, into the hot oil, mashing down the cakes to about ¼ inch. When the bottom side is brown, turn over and cook the other side. Be careful, they can scorch and burn easily. Once both sides are cooked, allow the cakes to drain on a paper towel to absorb any extra oil. Serve in place of mashed potatoes or French fries.

Feeds: 3-4

Notes:

FRIED POTATOES WITH ONIONS

This recipe is actually a hybrid cross between French fries and hash browns.

Tools needed:
Large frying pan
Potato peeler
Large spatula
Sharp knife

Ingredients:
4 or 5 medium potatoes
1 small onion, diced into very small pieces
Vegetable cooking oil

Add about 1cup of cooking oil to a frying pan and place the frying pan onto the stove, turning the eye just past medium. Peel the potatoes and dice into pieces about the size of a dice. Mix with the onion and add slowly to the hot oil. After about five minutes, turn and stir the potatoes, allowing to them to cook for several more minutes before you turn and stir again. Once the potatoes are brown, place them onto a paper towel on a plate and add salt to taste.

Feeds: about 3 or 4

Notes:

SPAGHETTI

This is one my all time favorite foods. I love authentic spaghetti made from scratch but that takes a lot of time and ingredients. Modern science has given us packaged noodles and canned sauce and it's not really bad. I like modern science.

Tools needed:
Large frying pan
Large sauce pan
Large fork
Colander
Large spoon

Ingredients:
1 pound of ground beef
1 can of spaghetti sauce
1 small package of spaghetti noodles
1 tablespoon of butter
Shredded mozzarella cheese

Place thawed ground beef in the frying pan on the stove, turning the eye up to about ¾ to high. Add four cups of water to a large saucepan and place the saucepan on the stove, turning the eye up to high. Add just a few drops of cooking oil and a dash of salt to the water. Brown the ground beef, tearing it into pieces with the large fork as it cooks. Once the water is boiling, add the noodles, allowing it to continue to boil. Once the ground beef is fully cooked, remove from heat. Pour the beef into a colander and rinse well with warm water. You are attempting to remove as much grease as possible. You can also rinse out the frying pan. Once drained, add the beef back to the pan and return to the heat. Wash the colander because you will need it again for the noodles. Open and add the spaghetti sauce to the meat and allow the sauce and meat mixture to boil, stirring occasionally. Once boiling, lower the heat to low and continue to stir occasionally.

Check the noodles. You can make sure they are done in several ways. I prefer to pull a few noodles out and taste them but you can toss one up against the cabinet. If it sticks, it's done. Remove from heat, drain in the colander. Return the noodles to the pot and add butter. Now, take up the noodles separately on a plate. Add about ¼ cup of shredded mozzarella cheese to the top of the noodles and then add a few spoons full of sauce to taste. You can top that with shredded oregano cheese if you like. Serve warm with garlic bread and salad.

Feeds: 3-4

Notes:

SPINACH LINGUINE WITH CHICKEN BREAST AND RED SAUCE

This sounds complicated but it's not. It will impress just about anyone though. If you can make spaghetti, you can make this. The best part of this recipe is that it is better for you than the regular spaghetti.

Tools needed:
Large frying pan
Large sauce pan
Large fork
Colander
Large spoon

Ingredients:
1 pound of boneless chicken breast
1 can of spaghetti sauce
1 small package of thin spinach linguine noodles
1 tablespoon of butter
Shredded mozzarella cheese
1 tablespoon of olive oil or vegetable oil

Add about 1 tablespoon of olive oil or vegetable oil to the frying pan and place thawed chicken breast in the oil. Turn the eye up to just past half and place the pan on the heat. Add four cups of water to a large saucepan and place the saucepan on the stove, turning the eye up to high. Add just a few drops of cooking oil and a dash of salt. Brown the chicken breast evenly, slicing into halves after one side is cooked and turning over. Once the water is boiling, add the noodles, allowing it to continue to boil. Once the chicken breasts are fully cooked, add the spaghetti sauce and allow the sauce to boil, stirring occasionally. Once boiling, lower the heat to low and continue to stir occasionally. Check the noodles. You can make sure they are done in several ways. I prefer to pull a few noodles out and taste them but you can toss one up against the cupboard. If it sticks, it's done. Remove from heat, drain in the colander. Return the noodles to the pan and add butter. Now, take up the noodles separately on a plate. Add about ¼ cup of shredded mozzarella cheese to the top and then add a chicken breast and a few spoons full of sauce to taste. You can top that with shredded oregano cheese if you like. Serve warm with garlic bread and salad.

Feeds: 3-4

Notes:

CHILI

This is a typical man recipe. If you can't cook anything else, chili is perfect. You can make it spicy but if you have small kids, you probably want to make it mild and add hot sauce once it's in your own bowl.

Tools needed:
Large sauce pan
Large fork
Large spoon
Can opener

Ingredients:
1 pound of lean ground beef
2 regular sized cans of chili tomatoes
2 regular sized cans of chili beans
1 small onion diced

In a large sauce pan, brown the ground beef on medium high heat, shredding it with the large fork as it cooks. Once the beef is brown, drain off any excess grease using a colander. Rinse the beef with warm water and return to the sauce pan and then back to the heat. Open and add the tomatoes, allowing the mixture to boil. Once boiling, open and stir in the two cans of chili beans. Allow the chili, once again to boil. Stir and reduce the heat to low. Let the chili simmer for about thirty minutes, stirring occasionally. The longer it simmers, the better it will be. Serve warm. Add shredded cheese and sour cream if you'd like. Any leftover chili can be frozen and saved for chili dogs.

Feeds: 3-4

Notes:

HAMBURGER STEAKS

Tools needed:
Large frying pan
Spatula
Medium mixing bowl

Ingredients:
1 pound of lean ground beef
1 small onion coarsely chopped
1 tablespoon of steak sauce
1 teaspoon of garlic powder
1/8 teaspoon of salt and pepper

In a medium mixing bowl, mix the beef, onion, steak sauce, garlic powder, salt and pepper. Shape the beef into four equally sized patties and place into a frying pan. Place the frying pan onto the stove with the heat at about ¾ of the way to high. Once the juices start to flow from the top of the patty, turn over and cook the other side. You can slice the patty open gently to make sure the inside is completely cooked, which is when there is no pink left inside. Serve with mashed potatoes and salad or any other vegetables.

Feeds: 3- 4

Notes:

HOME MADE CHICKEN FINGERS

I'm not a big fan of chicken fingers from the frozen food section. This recipe makes chicken fingers taste more like home made fried chicken.

Tools needed:
Large frying pan
1 medium mixing bowl
1 small mixing bowl
Sharp knife
Tongs

Ingredients:
4 large chicken breasts sliced lengthwise into fingers
2 cups of flour
1 tablespoons of Italian seasoning
1/8 tablespoon of salt
1/8 tablespoon of pepper
1/8 tablespoon of garlic powder
2 eggs
½ cup buttermilk
1 teaspoon of Louisiana Red hot sauce
1 cup of vegetable oil

In a medium mixing bowl, mix the flour, Italian seasoning, salt, pepper and garlic powder. In the small mixing bowl, mix the egg, buttermilk and hot sauce very well. The hot sauce won't overpower the chicken but it does give it a little flavor.

Add 1 cup of vegetable oil to the frying pan and place the pan on an eye that has been turned on just past half way. One at a time, dunk the chicken pieces into the egg mixture and then coat well with the flour mixture. You may want to use two separate forks for this; one for the eggs mixture and one for the flour mixture. Once the oil is hot, add the coated chicken, one piece at a time to the hot oil. Do not turn the chicken until you can see the bottom parts of the sides starting to brown. Premature turning may allow the breading to come off. Once the bottom part of the sides begins looking brown, gently turn with tongs and cook the other side. Once browned all over, remove from the pan with tongs and place onto a paper towel to soak up any extra grease. Serve warm with ketchup, steak sauce, barbeque sauce or thousand- island dressing.

Feeds: 4- 5

Notes:

CHICKEN AND RICE CASSEROLE

Tools needed:
1 - 9x13 (or equivalent) casserole dish
One large spoon

Ingredients:
1 cup of uncooked white rice
2-3 boneless chicken breasts
1 can of condensed cream of chicken soup
1 package of onion soup mix
2 cups of water

    Preheat oven to 345 degrees. Spray the inside of the casserole dish with cooking spray. Add the uncooked rice and onion soup mix. Add the water and the soup mix stirring well. Lay the chicken breast on top of the rice mixture and sprinkle with just a dash of salt and pepper. Place in the preheated oven and bake for 1 hour and 35 minutes. Serve warm with vegetables.

Feeds: 4-5

Notes:

PORK CHOPS

Tools needed:
Large frying pan
Medium mixing bowl
Large fork
1 cup measuring cup

Ingredients:
5 boneless pork chops
1 cup of self rising flour
1/8 teaspoon of Italian seasoning
1/8 teaspoon of salt
1/8 teaspoon of pepper
1 cup of vegetable oil

Add 1 cup of vegetable oil to a large frying pan and place on the stove with the eye turned on just past half way to high. In a medium mixing bowl, combine flour, salt, pepper and Italian seasoning and mix well. Take one pork chop and roll it around in the flour mixture until coated well. Slowly add the pork chop to the hot oil and repeat with the other chops. You can gently lift the chops from the grease after four or five minutes to make sure that the bottom is browned. Be careful because the breading could fall off of the meat. Once it is brown, gently turn over and cook the other side. When completely browned but not burned, remove from the pan and place onto a paper towel to absorb any extra grease. Serve warm with mashed potatoes and English peas.

Feeds: 3

Notes:

MEAT LOAF

Some people scoff at the idea of meatloaf but it's always been a favorite at my house.

Tools needed:
5 x 9 loaf or casserole pan (glass is ok)
Large mixing bowl
Large fork
½ cup measuring cup
1 cup measuring cup

Ingredients:
1 ½ pound of ground beef
1 cup of dried bread crumbs, crumbled
1 medium onion, diced coarsely
1 egg
¼ cup of steak sauce
¼ cup of ketchup
1/8 teaspoon of salt
1/8 teaspoon of pepper
1/8 teaspoon of Italian seasoning

Preheat oven to 350 degrees. Spray the inside of the pan with cooking spray. In a large bowl, combine the thawed ground beef, bread crumbs, egg, steak sauce, ketchup, salt, pepper, Italian seasoning and onion. Mix well by hand. Toss it into the pan and shape into a loaf with the edges not quite touching the sides. Cook in the oven for 1 hour. After an hour, turn off the heat and remove the meat loaf with a hot pad. Now generously coat the top of the meat loaf with ketchup and return to the warm oven for about ten minutes. Serve warm with cheesy potatoes and green beans.

Feeds: 3-4

Notes:

BEEF SKIZZLE

This may not sound good but it is one of my favorite meals. It's quick, cheap and easy.

Tools needed:
Large skillet
Large fork
½ cup measuring cup
Colander

Ingredients needed:
1 pound of lean ground beef
2 regular sized or one large size (15oz) can of pork and beans
1 small onion diced into small pieces
¼ cup of ketchup
Sour cream
Shredded cheese
Hot sauce
1/8 teaspoon of salt
1/8 teaspoon of pepper

Add the ground beef to a large skillet (frying pan), place on the oven with the eye ¾ of the way to high. Brown the beef, shredding as it cooks. Once all of the ground beef is brown, remove from heat and rinse with warm water using the colander. This will remove a lot of the excess grease.

Return the beef to the stove and add the pork and beans, onions, ketchup, salt and pepper. Allow the mixture to begin to boil then reduce the heat to low. Continue stirring often as the dish will begin to sizzle in the skillet (thus the name "skizzle"). Continue cooking on low for ten minutes and serve warm with a dab of sour cream, a sprinkling of shredded cheese and hot sauce to taste.

Feeds: 3-4

Notes:

COLE SLAW

This is a good side dish for just about anything. I like it with fish, meat loaf or even chicken.

Tools needed:
A hand held shredder/grater
A big knife
¼ cup measuring cup
1 teaspoon
Large mixing bowl

Ingredients:
1 medium sized green cabbage
Mayonnaise
Sweet pickle relish
Dill pickle juice
½ small onion

Cut the cabbage into three or four sections. In a large bowl, begin shredding the lettuce using firm back and forth motions on the grater. Be careful not to add fingers or finger nails to the recipe inadvertently. Hold the cabbage by the stem or the core but do not use the core. Once the cabbage is shredded, use a smaller part of the shredder to shred the onion into small pieces right on top of the shredded cabbage.

Now, and ¼ cup of sweet pickle relish and ¼ cup of dill pickle juice and two teaspoons of mayonnaise. Mix well and refrigerate for at least ½ hour before serving. Serve cold with fish or, my all time favorite, black eyed peas and fried potatoes. Leftovers will keep in the refrigerator for several days. This slaw is great for slaw dogs!

Feeds: 4-5

Notes:

HUSHPUPPIES

I always tend to make too many of these when I cook but the best part is that they are just as good cold, dipped in ketchup as they are warm with fish.

Tools needed:
Medium frying pan
Large fork
Tongs
Medium mixing bowl
Teaspoon

Ingredients:
1 cup of corn meal
½ cup of milk
1 egg
1 small onion, diced
2 cups of vegetable oil

Add 2 cups of vegetable oil to a medium frying pan. Place the pan on the stove and turn the eye just past medium. In a mixing bowl, combine all ingredients, stirring well. It should be about as thick as an extra-thick milkshake. Using a teaspoon, slowly spoon the batter one drop at a time into the hot oil. As the hushpuppies begin to brown, use the tongs to turn them over and cook evenly on both sides. Serve warm with fish. Leftovers can be enjoyed later dipped in ketchup.

Feeds: 4-5

Notes:

CORNBREAD

Tools needed:
Medium mixing bowl
Large cast iron skillet
1 cup measuring cup
¼ cup measuring cup
Table spoon
Large fork

Ingredients:
2 cups of corn meal
1 ½ cup of buttermilk
¼ cup of cooking oil
1 tablespoon of regular sugar
1 egg

Preheat oven to 390 degrees. Grease the bottom and inside of the cast iron skillet and place it in the oven to preheat. In a medium mixing bowl, combine all ingredients, stirring well with the large fork. Make sure all ingredients are well mixed all of the way down to the bottom. Corn meal has a way of hiding from buttermilk. Remove the cast iron skillet from the oven after about ten minutes with an oven mitt or hot pad. Pour the mixture into the skillet and place back in the oven. Bake for 30 minutes. You can check to make sure it is done by placing a butter knife through the top of the corn bread. If it comes out clean, it's done. If corn meal remains on the knife, let it cook a few more minutes. Serve warm with butter melted on top.

Feeds: 4-5

Notes:

MEXICAN CORNBREAD

This is a variation of the regular cornbread. I can eat it by itself. I can eat it by myself. I don't like to share my Mexican cornbread.

Tools needed:
Medium mixing bowl
Large cast iron skillet
1 cup measuring cup
¼ cup measuring cup
Table spoon
Large fork

Ingredients:
1 3/4 cups of corn meal
1 ½ cup of buttermilk
¼ cup of cooking oil
1 can of sweet whole kernel corn, drained
½ cup of mild salsa
½ cup of shredded cheddar cheese
1 egg

Preheat oven to 390 degrees. Grease the bottom and inside of the cast iron skillet and place it in the oven to preheat. In a medium mixing bowl, combine all ingredients, stirring well with the large fork. Make sure all ingredients are well mixed all of the way down to the bottom. Remember that the corn meal likes to hide from buttermilk. Remove the cast iron skillet from the oven after about ten minutes with an oven mitt or hot pad. Pour the mixture into the skillet and place back in the oven. Bake for 30 minutes. You can check to make sure it is done by placing a butter knife through the top of the corn bread. If it comes out clean, it's done. If corn meal remains on the knife, let it cook a few more minutes. Serve warm by itself or with any Tex-Mex meal.

Feeds: 4-5

Notes:

CORNBREAD MUFFINS

Tools needed:
Medium mixing bowl
Muffin pan
1 cup measuring cup
¼ cup measuring cup
Table spoon
Large fork

Ingredients:
1 ¾ cups of corn meal
¼ cup of self rising flour
1 ½ cup of buttermilk
¼ cup of cooking oil
1 tablespoon of regular sugar
1 egg

Preheat oven to 390 degrees. Generously spray the ports of the muffin pan. In a medium mixing bowl, combine all ingredients, stirring well with the large fork. Make sure all ingredients are well mixed all of the way down to the bottom. The corn meal needs to find the buttermilk and sometimes needs some help. Spoon the batter into the ports of the muffin pan to the point where it is about ¾ of the way full. Bake for 30 minutes. You can check to make sure it is done by placing a butter knife through the top of the corn bread. If it comes out clean, it's done. If corn meal remains on the knife, let it cook a few more minutes. Serve warm with butter melted on top. This is a great way to get the kids to eat corn bread. You may even be able to sneak in a few black eyed peas.

Feeds: 4-5

Notes:

CUBED STEAK

Tools needed:
Large frying pan
Large fork
Small mixing bowl
Medium mixing bowl

Ingredients:
4 or 5 cubed steaks
One egg
1 cup of milk
2 cups of flour
1/8 teaspoon of salt
1/8 teaspoon of pepper
1/8 teaspoon of garlic powder
1/8 teaspoon of Italian seasoning
1 cup of vegetable oil

Add 1 cup of vegetable oil to the frying pan and place it on the stove. Turn the eye just past medium.

In a medium mixing bowl, combine the flour, salt, pepper, garlic powder and Italian seasoning, mixing well. In the small mixing bowl, beat together the egg and milk. One at a time, dunk the cubed steak into the milk mixture then roll it into the flour mixture covering well. Slowly add each steak to the hot oil. Once the bottom side of the steak is browned, gently turn over with the large fork, being careful not to allow any of the breading to come off. Serve warm with potatoes and salad.

Feeds: 3-4

Notes:

BROWN GRAVY

There is a no secret to making gravy. Or, if there is, it's very closely guarded. Sometimes the gravy will come out perfect, others it may be lumpy or thin. Don't give up. Keep trying. Gravy makes everything better no matter what. Gravy is good. Gravy is good.

Tools needed:
Small sauce pan
Wooden (preferably) spoon

Ingredients:
7 tablespoons of butter (drippings from cooking bacon or sausage can also be used)
7 tablespoons of self rising flour
A dash of salt
A dash of pepper
2 cups of water

Turn on the small eye on the stove to just past half way. Melt the butter. As soon as the butter is melted, remove the pan from the eye and slowly add the flour, salt and pepper mixing together to a thin past. Add ¼ cup of water, mixing until that is pasty. Return the pan to the eye, stirring often. Once the mixture starts to become thick, add another ½ cup of water and stir. Repeat this step until all of the water has been used. Be careful not to let the mixture boil or scorch. Once all of the water has been used, continue to stir until the gravy thickens. Remove from heat and serve on top of mashed potatoes, cubed steak or beef liver.

Feeds: 3-5

Notes:

BURRITOS

This is another recipe that I "allow" my wife to cook. It's simple this way and takes a lot of the guess work out of assembling the burrito.

Tools needed:
Large skillet (frying pan)
Large fork
3 teaspoons
Knife
Colander

Ingredients:
1 pound of lean ground beef
1 regular size can of refried beans
1 regular jar of mild salsa
Chili powder
Sour cream
Shredded cheese
Lettuce
Tomato
Flour tortillas

In a large skillet, brown the ground beef on an eye that is turned on to ¾ of the way to high. Shred the beef with the large fork as it browns. While this is cooking, shred ½ of a head of lettuce and dice one large tomato. Once the ground beef is cooked, rinse thoroughly with warm water using the colander.

Return the beef to the stove. Add a dash of chili powder, 1/3 of the jar of salsa and the whole can of refried beans. Stir the ingredients together for several minutes before reducing the heat to low.

Sprinkle shredded cheese into a tortilla and warm for about 15 seconds in the microwave. Remove from the microwave and spoon about two tablespoons of the beef and bean mixture onto the tortilla. Add a teaspoon or two of sour cream, a handful of lettuce and some tomato to taste. Add hot sauce or salsa if needed. Wrap and enjoy.

Feeds: 3-4

Notes:

TACO SALAD

This is great for people who want to sneak a salad in every now and again. It's Tex-Mex food without the guilt.

Tools needed:
Large skillet (frying pan)
Large fork
3 teaspoons
Knife
Colander
Salad bowls

Ingredients:
1 pound of lean ground beef
1 regular size can of refried beans
1 regular jar of mild salsa
Chili powder
Ranch dressing
Shredded cheese
Lettuce
Tomato
Corn chips or tortilla chips

In a large skillet, brown the ground beef on an eye that is turned on to ¾ of the way to high. Shred the beef with the large fork as it browns. While this is cooking, cut the lettuce up by hand into small bite sized pieces and dice one large tomato. Once the ground beef is cooked, rinse thoroughly with warm water using the colander.

Return the beef to the stove. Add a dash of chili powder, half of the jar of salsa and the whole can of refried beans. Stir the ingredients together for several minutes before reducing the heat to low.

In a large salad bowl, cover the bottom well with corn chips then layer on lettuce, a handful of tomatoes, 1/8 cup of shredded cheese and two tablespoons of the beef mixture. Repeat at least once more. Add more salsa if desired and ranch dressing. Jalapeno peppers can also be added for a kick.

Feeds: 3-4

Notes:

PO MAMA STEW

My mama, rest her soul, could make anything taste good. This is a recipe that we all seemed to love growing up. It's easy to cook and it falls under the heading of "hearty".

Tools needed:
A large sauce pan
A large fork
Potato peeler
Knife
Colander
Teaspoon
One cup measuring cup

Ingredients:
1 pound of lean ground beef (ground turkey could also be used)
5 medium potatoes
1 regular sized can of English peas
1/8 teaspoon of salt
1/8 teaspoon of pepper
1/8 teaspoon of Italian seasoning
1 teaspoon of Worcestershire sauce
2 cups of water

In a large sauce pan, brown the ground beef over medium heat, shredding as it cooks with the large fork. While the beef cooks, peel five medium potatoes, dicing each into pieces no larger than a golf ball. Once the beef is browned, rinse the beef well with warm water using the colander.

Return the beef to the pan on the stove. Add one can of English peas including the water. Add the potatoes, salt, pepper, Italian seasoning, Worcestershire sauce and two cups of water. Allow this to begin to boil, stirring often. After the stew begins to boil, lower the heat to low and allow the stew to simmer for about 45 minutes.

Now, take three teaspoons of flour and place into the one cup measuring cup, adding four teaspoons of water. Mix this into a paste and then add the paste to the stew to thicken the stew. Stir often until thickened. Serve warm with homemade biscuits or fresh bread.

Feeds: 3-5

Notes:

SALMON PATTIES

Tools needed:
A large skillet
Large fork
Small spatula
Knife

Ingredients:
1 regular sized can of pink salmon
1 egg
½ cup of corn meal
½ cup of flour
1 small onion, diced
1/8 teaspoon of salt
1/8 teaspoon of pepper
1/8 teaspoon of Italian seasoning
½ cup of vegetable oil

Add ½ cup of oil to the skillet and place on the stove. Turn the eye to medium. While the oil is heating, add together the salmon, egg, flour, corn meal, onion, salt, pepper and Italian seasoning. Mix well using the large fork.

Using a tablespoon, measure out the salmon and place into the hot oil. As one side browns, gently turn with the small spatula. Once completely and evenly browned, remove the patties from the oil and allow to drain on a paper towel. Serve warm with cheesy macaroni and a vegetable. I like to add just a dash of hot sauce to the patties once cooked.

Feeds: 3-5

Notes:

KRAUT AND WEENIES

This is such a simple recipe but it sure is good.

Tools needed:
Medium sauce pan
Knife
Tablespoon

Ingredients:
1 pack of all meat wieners
1 can of sauerkraut
1 tablespoon of brown sugar

In a medium sauce pan, pour in the sauerkraut and gently sprinkle with one tablespoon of brown sugar. Place the pan on the stove with the eye turned on to medium heat. Cover and let the sauerkraut heat up for about five minutes.

Cut the wieners into small pieces, about three or four pieces for each wiener. Add the wieners to the pan with the sauerkraut, stirring to combine. Cover and cook for ten minutes stirring at least twice. Remove from heat and allow the recipe to stand for about five minutes before serving warm with cheesy macaroni or even biscuits.

Feeds: 4-5

Notes:

HOT WINGS

Back when I was a single dad, I used to make hot wings almost every Saturday. I'd eat them until I couldn't stand myself.

Tools needed:
Large sauce pan
Large casserole dish
Large mixing bowl
¼ cup measuring cup
1 cup measuring cup
Tongs

Ingredients:
3 pounds of frozen chicken wings, thawed
½ cup of red hot sauce
½ cup of butter
3 tablespoons of vinegar
4 cups of vegetable oil

Heat the vegetable oil in the sauce pan with the eye ¾ of the way to high. Preheat the oven to 350 degrees. Rinse the wings well and pat dry with a paper towel. Slowly add the wings, one at a time to the oil. They may crackle and pop so be careful. The oil should always be just a little bit higher than the wings to allow the wings to cook evenly. After about ten minutes, the wings should be done.

In a large mixing bowl, combine the hot sauce, butter and vinegar. A dash of cayenne pepper can be added here if you prefer your wings hotter.

Add the cooked wings to the hot sauce, turning well to make sure the wings are coated. Once the wings are coated, spread them out onto a cookie sheet. Place the cookie sheet into the oven for another 7 to 10 minutes to allow the wings to soak in the hot sauce. Serve warm with a side of ranch dressing and celery.

Feeds: 3-4

Notes:

BLACK EYED PEAS

My favorite meal of all time would have to be black eyed peas, cole slaw, fried potatoes and corn bread. Call me country but just don't call me late for supper.

Tools needed:
Large sauce pan
Large spoon

Ingredients:
8 slices of bacon or a small ham hock
4 cups of water
1 small bag of dried black eyed peas
1/8 teaspoon of salt
1/8 teaspoon of pepper
1/8 teaspoon of oregano

Add the bacon to the large sauce pan. Place the pan on the oven on high heat. Allow the bacon to just get warm enough to sizzle and slowly add four cups of water. Rinse the peas using a colander, checking for any small rocks or stems. Add the black eyed peas to the boiling water along with the salt, pepper and oregano. Continue to boil for about ten minutes stirring occasionally. Reduce the heat to low and cover. Let the pot simmer for about 2 and one-half hours. Serve warm with rice or slaw and fried potatoes.

Feeds: 3-4

Notes:

PINTO BEANS

Tools needed:
Large sauce pan
Large spoon

Ingredients:
8 slices of bacon or a small ham hock
4 cups of water
1 small bag of dried pinto beans
1 small onion, diced
1/8 teaspoon of salt
1/8 teaspoon of pepper

    Add the bacon to the large sauce pan. Place the pan on the oven on high heat. Allow the bacon to just get warm enough to sizzle and slowly add four cups of water. Rinse the beans using a colander, checking for any small rocks or stems. Add the beans to the boiling water along with the salt, pepper and onions. Continue to boil for about ten minutes stirring occasionally. Reduce the heat to low and cover. Let the pot simmer for about 2 and ½ hours. Serve warm with rice or slaw and fried potatoes.

Feeds: 3-4

Notes:

VEGGIE SOUP

The recipe for vegetable soup changes from state to state, from family to family and from generation to generation. I would estimate that there are probably 10,000 different recipes out there for this one simple meal. This is the 10,001st. I like them all.

Tools needed:
Large stock pot
Potato peeler
Knife
Large spoon
Large fork
½ cup measuring cup
1 cup measuring cup
Colander

Ingredients:
1 pound of ground beef
1 medium onion, diced
2 potatoes, diced
1 can of small carrots
1 can of whole kernel corn
½ cup frozen okra
1 can of green beans
1 can of whole tomatoes
½ teaspoon of salt
½ teaspoon of pepper
1/8 teaspoon of oregano
1/8 teaspoon of garlic powder
2 cups of water

In a large stock pot, brown the ground beef on an eye that is turned up to ¾ to high. Once browned, drain excess grease using a colander. Return the beef to the pot; add tomatoes and onions, stirring to allow the tomatoes to cook down. After about five minutes, add the water and allow the soup to boil. Once boiling, add the potatoes, the whole can of corn, carrots and green beans including the water then add the okra, salt, pepper, oregano and garlic powder. Allow this to begin to boil, stirring occasionally. Once it does start to boil, lower the heat to low, cover and allow to simmer for an hour, stirring occasionally. Serve warm with cornbread or peanut butter and jelly sandwiches. Freeze leftovers for a cold rainy day.

Feeds: 5-6

Notes:

FRIED CHICKEN LIVERS

When my oldest son was serving in Iraq, I asked him what he wanted to eat when he came home. He said chicken livers. He could have asked for a huge steak and all the trimmings and I would have been glad to oblige but he asked for chicken livers and that is what he got. Let's pray that all of our troops around the world get to come home to their favorite meals safe and sound.

Tools needed:
Large frying pan
Fork
Tongs
Medium mixing bowl

Ingredients:
2 pounds of fresh chicken livers, rinsed and drained
2 cups of vegetable oil
2 cups of flour
1/8 teaspoon of salt
1/8 teaspoon of pepper
1/8 teaspoon of garlic powder
1/8 teaspoon of poultry seasoning

Add the vegetable oil to the frying pan and place on an eye turned to just past half way. Add the flour, salt, pepper, garlic powder and poultry seasoning together in a medium mixing bowl. Drop the livers into the flour mixture one at a time, rolling into the flour to coat completely. Then place the coated livers slowly into the hot oil. Be careful because chicken livers have been known to pop and spatter like the last lap of the Daytona 500. Keep the livers turned in the oil with the tongs, allowing them to brown well. The livers should be crisp on the outside but tender on the inside. Serve warm with mashed potatoes and peas or just dip in ketchup and enjoy.

Feeds: 2-3 soldiers and their proud Dads

Notes:

BEEF LIVER WITH ONION GRAVY

When I was a student at Troup High School in LaGrange, Georgia, they still served liver and gravy at lunch. That was always my lucky day because I always got everyone else's liver. I've always liked liver. I think it's good for you. I just like the taste. Try it just once this way.

Tools needed:
Large frying pan
Large fork
Medium mixing bowl
Knife
½ cup measuring cup
1 cup measuring cup
Tablespoon

Ingredients:
1 ½ pounds of fresh calf liver
2 cups of flour
2 cups of water
1/8 teaspoon of salt
1/8 teaspoon of pepper
1/8 teaspoon of poultry seasoning
1 ½ cup of vegetable oil

In a large frying pan, heat the oil on an eye turned to just past halfway. Rinse the liver and pat dry with paper towels. In a mixing bowl combine the flour, salt, pepper and poultry seasoning, mixing well. Add the liver to the flour one piece at a time, rolling in the flour to make sure it's covered well. Slowly place the liver in the hot oil one at a time. Be careful because it may splatter and pop. Once the liver is browned on both sides, place on a paper towel to drain extra grease off.

Once all of the liver is cooked, drain off all but about ¼ cup of the remaining grease from the pan. Lower the heat to medium. Add in the chopped onion, a dash of salt and a dash of pepper. Next, add 2 tablespoons of flour, mixing with the grease and onions until pasty. Add ½ cup of water, stirring constantly. Once this thickens, add another ½ cup of water. Continue stirring and then add the liver back into the gravy, simmering on low for another five minutes. Serve warm with mashed potatoes and English peas.

Feeds: 3-4

Notes:

GRILLED STEAK

I make this recipe using a gas grill. It's even better on charcoal but it's not quite as convenient. Whichever grill you choose, be careful and follow all of the safety rules. Please watch small children carefully.

Tools needed:
Grill
Large fork
Casserole dish

Ingredients:
2 pounds of steak (I prefer rib eye, but I've eaten plenty of round steak in my past)
Soy sauce
1/8 teaspoon of salt
1/8 teaspoon of pepper
1/8 teaspoon of garlic powder

In a large casserole dish, arrange the steak into one layer. Drizzle lightly with soy sauce and sprinkle with the salt, pepper and garlic powder. Now go and start the grill while the steaks are soaking in the spices.

Once the grill is hot, add the steaks to the grill. Once the juices begin to flow from the top, it's time to flip. There's really no easy way to tell you how long to cook for medium rare or well done. The best advice I can give you is to sacrifice. Yep, hopefully you bought one extra steak and this one will be sacrificed as you cook. Slice off pieces as you cook to sample the doneness. That really is my secret to cooking the perfect steak. It takes sacrifice. Serve hot with a loaded baked potato and salad.

Feeds: 3-4 depending on how much sacrifice you had to make

Notes:

FRIED FISH

Tools needed:
Large frying pan
Tongs
Medium mixing bowl

Ingredients:
1 ½ pound of fresh or thawed fish fillets
1 ½ cups of flour
½ cup of corn meal
1/8 teaspoon of salt
1/8 teaspoon of pepper
2 cups of vegetable oil

In a large frying pan, heat the oil on an eye turned up to just past halfway. Rinse and pat dry using a paper towel. In a mixing bowl, add the flower, salt and pepper, mixing well. Gently roll the fish through the flour, coating completely. Add the fish slowly to the hot oil. Once the bottom of the fish is golden brown, use the tongs to gently turn the fish over. Once both sides are cooked, take up the fish and allow it to drain on a paper towel. Serve hot with hushpuppies and cole slaw.

Feeds: 3-4

Notes:

BAKED FISH

I first started baking fish to be more healthy but then I realized that I kind of like it that way. My recipe uses Italian dressing to give it a little zest.

Tools needed:
Large casserole dish
Spatula

Ingredients:
1 ½ pounds fresh or thawed fish fillets
½ cup of regular Italian dressing
1/8 teaspoon of salt

Preheat oven to 325 degrees. Generously spray the bottom of the casserole dish. Arrange the fish fillets inside the dish. Drizzle with Italian seasoning and then sprinkle with salt. Bake for 20 minutes. Serve hot with a pasta dish or rice.

Feeds: 3-4

Notes:

DESSERTS

DESSERTS

I don't remember having desert much as a child but I do remember birthday cakes. I was the youngest of five sons and all of our birthdays fell within a two and a half week window starting in late June. During those heavenly days of summer, we ate cake. My birthday was first so I chose white cake with caramel icing. The other brothers chose yellow cake with chocolate icing, white cake with strawberry icing, chocolate cake with chocolate icing, German chocolate cake or any of the other combinations that Mom could dream up.

Today, I still like cake but I have never cooked one from scratch and probably never will. With three new babies, I don't think I could find the time or patience to do what mom did. And who would want to. The stuff comes in boxes now as a mix. The icing even comes in those cute little tubs. They have butter cream icing, five different types of chocolate and even lemon and cherry icing.

I have said it before and I will say it again. Make it simple because there is no way to Relax if it's complicated. Let them eat cake and let it be from a box!

BIRTHDAY CAKE

This is as simple as it gets. I am sorry if it's too simple. My intentions are to make it simple enough to allow any man, no matter how well versed he may be in the kitchen, to cook a cake for his family and cherish a memory.

Tools needed:
2 eight inch cake pans
One mixing bowl
Whisk
Large spoon
Butter knife

Ingredients:
1 box of cake mix
Whatever else they tell you on the box, normally oil, water and eggs
1 container of icing

In the kitchen, read the box. Follow the directions. Bake the cake. Once the cake has cooled, spoon out about a third of the icing onto the bottom layer and spread evenly. Now, place the second layer on top. Use the knife to spoon out a little icing at a time to spread over the sides of the cake. Then add the remaining icing on the top, spreading evenly. Use the broad side of the knife to make designs in the icing on top. This makes them think it was expensive or time consuming. Serve with ice cream or serve alone.

Feeds: 6-10

Notes:

CUPCAKES

Cupcakes are a lot like the wide ties that we sometimes wear. They keep going in and out of fashion. The new generation of cupcakes is astounding. You can buy them at bakeries now that actually specialize in cupcakes. These can be monuments to their baker and also serve as shrines to their consumer. I like them a lot but I also like to bake cupcakes at home with the babies to enjoy some family time. Its cheap entertainment and the results provide immediate and long term sweetness.

Tools needed:
Cupcake pan
Paper cupcake cups
Mixing bowl
Whisk
Spoon

Ingredients:
1 box of cake mix
Whatever else they tell you on the box, normally oil, water and eggs
1 container of icing
Sprinkles

Place the paper cups in the cupcake pan and follow the directions for making a cake on the box. Spoon the batter into the cup cake cups until they are about ¾ of the way full. Bake. When they are cooled, ice them and decorate with sprinkles.

Feeds: 10-12

Notes:

SUGAR COOKIES

This book is about being simple. If you used the previous recipes for cake or cupcakes, you know how simple I can make it. Well, this recipe is even simpler. In the frozen food section at the grocery store, they sell sugar cookies. They're already mixed and ready to cook. That's the recipe. While you are there, get some cookie cutters for design and enjoy making fun shaped sugar cookies with the kids. Add sprinkles or glitter and white icing, colored with simple food coloring after the cookies are done if you would like. Make a memory, don't make a hassle.

Tools needed:
Cookie sheet
Spatula
Cookie cutter

Ingredients:
You and your kids
A tube of frozen cookie dough
Sprinkles, glitter and smiles

Follow the directions on the container. Make sure that you are careful with small children around a hot oven. Have fun and Relax!

Feeds: 5-6 depending on how they react to sugar

Notes:

HOLIDAYS

HOLIDAYS

Growing up, we didn't have a whole lot of material things. Christmas gifts were never wrapped because all of the money was spent on the few gifts we received. We were happy, though, for what Santa brought on Christmas morning.

I think the cheer on Christmas morning, also, came from waking up to the smell of Christmas dinner being cooked. There were seven of us until marriage brought first one then two and then three sisters-in-law to the table. That was a lot of food for mom to cook. But she started early and kept going right up until it was time to eat.

There was potato salad, a turkey, a ham, several casseroles, green beans, sweet potatoes, rolls, dumplings, cranberry sauce and my favorite, cornbread dressing. I can still taste it.

I've been chasing mom's recipe for years. She never wrote it down anywhere but it tasted just as good every year.

As I grew up and became a single dad, I normally sent the kids off to their mother's family because I knew there would be a large family gathered around a big table with lots of food. I wanted them to have, at least in spirit, what I had.

But, one year, I decided to give Christmas dinner a try myself. It wasn't spectacular. We had ham and potato salad and green beans and cranberry sauce and my first pan of cornbread dressing.

I miss my mom. I think she would be happy that I tried and she'd be proud that I continued to try until I almost have it right. Just one more year.

ALMOST MOM'S CORNBREAD DRESSING

Making cornbread dressing from scratch takes time. This is not the simple either. But it is worth it. I have made the boxed stuffing from the store and it's good but it just doesn't compare with the real thing.

Tools needed:
Large mixing bowl
Large casserole dish
Knife
Large fork

Ingredients:
1 pan of cornbread (see the recipe in the dinner section)
4 regular hamburger or hot dog buns, torn into very small pieces
1 large onion, diced
2 cups of chicken broth
1 cube of chicken bouillon, dissolved in 1/4 cup warm water
1 can of cream of celery soup
4 eggs
½ teaspoon of salt
1 teaspoon of pepper
1 teaspoon of garlic powder
½ teaspoon of poultry seasoning
3 tablespoons of cooking oil

Preheat the oven to 350 degrees. Spray the inside of a large casserole pan with cooking spray.

In a large mixing bowl, add the cornbread and the buns, breaking up as much as possible. Add the diced onion, chicken broth, soup and dissolved chicken bouillon. Mix well. Now add the eggs, salt, pepper, garlic powder, poultry seasoning and cooking oil. Mix again, making sure that all dry ingredients become moist. If the mixture is too dry and doesn't seem to be sticking together well, you can add a little more chicken broth.

Bake at 350 degrees for 45 minutes, or until the top is brown. Serve warm with love.

Feeds: 5-6

Notes:

TURKEY

Cooking a turkey is a lot easier than most people think. You can bake it in the oven or you can fry it. I have never fried a turkey because I have seen too many internet videos of those who tried and failed. Always follow the cooking directions on the turkey label. That label will tell you how long to cook the bird and what temperature to cook it with. The key is prep and follow-through.

Tools needed:
1 large disposable roasting pan (the cheap aluminum kind)
A roll of aluminum foil
A large fork
A knife

Ingredients:
Big turkey, thawed completely
3 sticks of butter
1 teaspoon of salt
1 teaspoon of pepper
1 teaspoon of garlic powder
1 teaspoon of poultry seasoning

Preheat the oven to 325 degrees.

If the turkey is completely thawed, the bag of gizzards and livers the poultry processing plant puts on the inside of the bird will come out completely without too much effort. Rinse the turkey and pat dry with a paper towel. Before you place the turkey in the roasting pan, hold it up so that its legs are pointed straight up. Sprinkle half of all the seasonings inside the bird and place a whole stick of butter inside as well. Lay the turkey in the pan, breast side up. Rub the outside with ½ of a stick of butter and sprinkle the rest of the seasoning on the outside.

Loosely cover the turkey with aluminum foil and place the turkey in the oven. Mark your time. Cook only as long as the recommendation on the label. Once every 45 minutes, remove the turkey from the oven and rub the outside with another half stick of butter. If you run out of butter, just use a spoon and drizzle the turkey broth from the turkey over the outside. With 45 minutes left before the turkey is done according to the recommendation on the label, remove the aluminum foil to allow the exterior to brown.

Serve warm with cornbread dressing, cranberry sauce, stuffed eggs and green beans. This is one of my all time favorite meals.

Feeds 5-6 with plenty left over for sandwiches

Notes:

STUFFED EGGS

My four year old daughter takes after me in tastes. She even likes stuffed eggs. Too much.

Tools needed:
Medium sauce pan
Knife
Fork
Teaspoon
Small mixing bowl

Ingredients:
6 large eggs
1 teaspoons of pickle relish
2 teaspoons of mayonnaise
½ teaspoon of mustard
1/8 teaspoon of salt

Turn an eye on to high. In a medium to large sauce pan, add the six eggs carefully. Now add enough water to cover the eggs. Add a dash of salt (this supposedly helps to keep the eggs from cracking). Let the eggs boil for 5-7 minutes. Remove from heat and rinse with cold water for about a minute.

Peel the eggs carefully and split each egg into equal halves with a sharp knife. Place the yellows in the small mixing bowl. Add pickle relish, mayonnaise, mustard and salt to the yellows, mixing and mashing with a fork. Now, spoon this mixture back into the open white halves. Refrigerate and serve with any holiday meal.

Feeds: Me and Maggie and maybe one more person. May feed 6-8 any other time.

Notes:

HAM

Just like the recipe for turkey earlier in this chapter, ham is an easy recipe. Just follow the recommendation on the label for cooking temperature and cooking time. What sets my recipe apart if the prep and follow-through.

Tools needed:
1 large disposable roasting pan
1 roll of aluminum foil
Large fork
Knife
Medium mixing bowl
½ cup measuring cup
1 table spoon
1 teaspoon

Ingredients:
Large ham, thawed completely
1 ½ cups of honey
2 tablespoons of mustard
1 teaspoon of garlic powder

Preheat the oven to the recommended temperature on the label. Different companies vary. Read the label. Unwrap the ham and place it into the large roasting pan.

Combine the honey, mustard and garlic powder in the mixing bowl, stirring well. Now, drizzle the outside of the ham with half of the honey glaze using the large spoon. Cover loosely with aluminum foil and begin cooking. Halfway through cooking, drizzle the other half of the honey glaze over the ham, cover and continue cooking. Then, with thirty minutes remaining in the cooking time, remove the ham from the oven and drench the ham with its own juices using a large spoon. Recover and continue cooking.

Serve warm with cold potato salad and green beans.

Feeds: 5 to 6 with plenty left over for ham sandwiches or ham and eggs.

Notes:

FIVE CUP SALAD

For me, this should be called five star salad because it tastes so good. The reason they call it five cup salad, by the way, is because it has five cups of ingredients. It's that easy.

Tools needed:
1 cup measuring cup
Large mixing bowl
Large spoon

Ingredients:
1 cup of shredded coconut
1 cup of maraschino cherries, drained
1 cup of mandarin oranges with juice
1 cup of sour cream
1 cup of mini marshmallows

Combine all ingredients in the large mixing bowl. Refrigerate for several hours and serve chilled as a dessert or snack.

Feeds: 5-6

Notes:

PARTIES

PARTIES

Most men will tell you that the best part of manhood is being able to just bring chips to the party. Well, wouldn't the women just swoon if you brought in something that you created yourself? Yep, you'd be the talk of the party, even if the creation isn't any good. You'd get credit for trying.

Well, here are a few dip recipes and some finger food recipes. They are all very easy to make and taste great.

PROENZA BEAN DIP

My wife's BFF got married recently and, with a new man came the best bean dip recipe I have ever tried. Spicy good!

Tools needed:
Very large mixing bowl
Frying pan
Knife
Large spoon

Ingredients:
2 pounds lean ground beef
3 cans of black eyed peas
1 can of kidney beans
2 cans of fire roasted diced tomatoes
4 jalapeño peppers, diced
1 bell pepper, diced
½ large onion, diced
3 tablespoons of minced garlic
2 teaspoons of salt
2 teaspoons of black pepper
2 ½ tablespoons of red pepper sauce
1 bottle of red wine vinaigrette dressing

Place a large frying pan on a large eye on the stove. Turn the heat to ¾ to high and add the ground beef. Shred with a large fork while cooking until the beef is brown. Drain the grease using a colander.

In a large bowl, add the beef and all of the ingredients. The whole contents of the canned peas, beans and tomatoes should be added including the liquid. Stir very well and refrigerate. Stir every hour to even out the spices. Serve chilled with tortilla chips.

Feeds: A lot but it goes fast.

Notes:

HACIENDA DIP

This is a simple recipe that is always a party favorite. Serve with tortilla or corn chips and watch it disappear.

Tools needed:
Frying pan
Large mixing bowl
Knife
Large fork
Large spoon

Ingredients:
1 pound of ground beef (or sausage if you want an extra kick)
1 pound of Velveeta cheese
1 jar of Picante sauce

Place a large frying pan on the stove and turn the eye to ¾ of the way to high. Add thawed ground beef. Cook the beef until brown, shredding well with the large fork. Drain the meat of any excess grease using a colander and rinsing with warm water.

In a large, microwave safe bowl, cube the Velveeta cheese into small pieces and add the picante sauce. Microwave on high for about one minute. Stir. If the cheese is still not melted, you may need to heat for a little longer just be careful not to scorch it. Once the cheese is melted, add the ground beef and mix well. Serve warm with tortilla chips or corn chips.

Feeds: a half dozen hombres

Notes:

SWEET SOUTHERN TEA

I was 22 years old the first time I visited Chicago. I was at a fancy restaurant. The waitress asked me what I wanted to drink and I said "sweet tea". She looked at me like I was from another planet. That is the first time that I really noticed the difference between the south and everyone else. If ya'll would just sit back and drink some cold sweet tea, life will seem a lot better.

Tools needed:
Medium sauce pan
One gallon pitcher
½ cup measuring cup

Ingredients:
4 regular black tea bags
1 regular bag of green tea
¼ cup cranberry juice
1 ¾ cup pure cane sugar

Turn an eye on the stove to high. Fill a medium sauce pan with water almost all of the way. Allow the water to start boiling and remove from heat. Add all five tea bags, swirling the bags in the water continuously while holding the strings. Do this for at least a few minutes. You'll see the water start to turn dark. Let the tea sit for another five minutes before swirling the bags a few more times. Throw the bags away and pour the warm tea into a one gallon pitcher. While the tea is warm, add the sugar and stir well. The sugar will dissolve completely in hot or warm tea. Add ¼ cup cranberry juice and stir. Fill the pitcher up the rest of the way with water. This tea taste good served over ice with any food or by itself on the front porch.

Servings: 10-12

Notes:

PLOPCORN

This is simple. You pop some popcorn in the microwave, add a few ingredients and plop down in your favorite chair with your favorite kids to watch their favorite movie.

Tools needed:
Large mixing bowl

Ingredients:
1 large bag of microwave popcorn, popped
1 small bag of M&Ms
About 1 cup of Honey Nut Cheerios or Apple Cinnamon Cheerios
About 1 cup of animal crackers or honey graham animal crackers

In a large bowl, combine all ingredients and shake the bowl to mix it up. Divide into smaller bowls and plop down on the couch with the kids. You can use Fruit Loops or Kix instead of Cheerios or Reese's Pieces instead of M&Ms. Mix and match and find your favorite.

Feeds: 3-4

Notes:

FRIED PICKLES

A lot of people have tried fried pickles in restaurants but very few have tried making these appetizers at home. It's a little complicated and you'll have to borrow a beer from a neighbor but it's worth it.

Tools needed:
2 medium mixing bowls
½ cup measuring cup
Teaspoon
Large fork
Tongs
Frying pan

Ingredients:
1 quart of thinly sliced dill pickles
2 cups of cooking oil
2 cups of flour
1 cup of beer
1 teaspoon of hot sauce
1 teaspoon of black pepper
1 teaspoon of garlic powder

Turn an eye on the oven to about ¾ of the way to high and add cooking oil. Make sure the oil isn't too high or it might splash out and cause a fire.

In one small mixing bowl, combine 1 cup of flour and 1 teaspoon of garlic powder. In the other bowl, combine 1 cup of flour, 1 cup of beer, 1 teaspoon of hot sauce and 1 teaspoon of black pepper. Mix the ingredients well to form a batter. Now, one at a time, roll a pickle in the dry flour and dunk it well in the batter, adding it immediately to the hot oil. Add several pickles to the hot oil at one time. There will be no need to turn the pickles if the oil is deep enough because when they are done, they'll float to the top. Just make sure that the batter is browned and be careful removing the pickles as the cooked batter may fall off at this stage. Allow to drain on a paper towel and serve with a side of ranch dressing and a side of chipotle sauce.

Feeds: 7-9

Notes:

SAUSAGE BALLS

This is always good for parties or office gatherings. When everyone expects you to just bring drinks and chips or the cups and plates, surprise everyone with this.

Tools needed:
Cookie sheet or casserole dish
Large mixing bowl
Large fork
Tablespoon
½ cup measuring cup

Ingredients:
1 pound roll of mild sausage
1 egg
1 cup of sharp cheddar cheese
A few shakes of grated parmesan cheese
2 ½ cups of flour

Preheat the oven to 345 degrees. Spay the inside of the casserole dish or cookie sheet with cooking spray. In a large mixing bowl, combine all of the ingredients, mixing very well. Shape the sausage into balls using the tablespoon. Place each sausage ball on the cookie sheet or in the casserole dish. Leave enough space between each so that they will not touch. The sausage balls will rise slightly during cooking. Bake at 345 degrees for about 20 minutes or until the sausage balls are brown. Allow to drain on a paper towel and serve warm.

Feeds: 8-10

Notes:

SALSA

This recipe can be adapted to almost any taste. I like it spicy. If you like it mild, leave out some of the hot peppers.

Tools needed:
Large mixing bowl
Large spoon
Sharp knife
Teaspoon
½ cup measuring cup

Ingredients:
3 large tomatoes, chopped
1 medium onion, diced
3 jalapeno peppers, diced
¼ teaspoon of oregano
1/8 teaspoon of chili powder
1 teaspoon of garlic powder
½ teaspoon of salt
3 teaspoons of vinegar

Mix all of the ingredients together well. Refrigerate. The ingredients will begin to come together after a couple of hours in the refrigerator. Serve with tortilla chips.

Feeds: 6-8

Notes:

FLIPPIN DIP

This is definitely not a recipe for kids because of the horseradish. It's also not a recipe for adults because of the jelly. I guess that's why it's called flippin dip. You flip back and forth between two worlds when you eat this. It's simple and good.

Tools needed:
Small sauce pan
Large spoon
Serving bowl

Ingredients:
1 regular 10 ounce jar of apple jelly
1 regular 10 ounce jar of pineapple preserves
1 regular five ounce jar of real horseradish

Turn the eye on the stove on to about half way to high. Combine all of the ingredients in a small sauce pan. Begin stirring even before you put it on the stove and keep stirring until all of the ingredients have melted together. Remove from heat and pour into a serving bowl. Refrigerate for at least an hour and serve with crackers and cream cheese.

Feeds: 10-12

Notes:

AND FINALLY

As I wrote this book, I was able to look back in time to parts of the last twenty-six years. I was able to remember Shanna and Bryant when they were young. And, ultimately, I was able to remember that I was young too.

One of the things I have always liked about family meals is that it provides a time for our children to make memories and to bond. I guess I never realized I was making memories and bonding as well.

While it was extremely tough to be a single dad with two small kids, it was also rewarding. If not for that difficult and wonderful time, I wouldn't have this book.

As a sophomore at Valdosta State University, I sat in a Public Relations class one day and the professor asked each of us if we ever wanted to publish a book. I was one of the first to raise a hand. He asked what I wanted to publish. Without thinking, I said that it would probably be a fiction novel about aliens and abductions. He chuckled. I chuckled.

Three decades later, I have finally written a book about abduction. This is it.

You see, I was abducted. I was abducted by little bitty aliens, one right after the other beginning in 1985. They did experiments on me like messing up their rooms, pitching temper tantrums and hiding notes from school. They also experimented with my heart. I wouldn't be the man I am today if it not for each of one those experiments. I hope they never stop.

ACKNOWLEDGEMENTS

Relax Dad is a registered trademark of The Gra'mag-dela Company.

"Relax Dad, It's Just the Kitchen" is the first in a series of books for men.

Relax Dad merchandise; including Relax Dad aprons, the book, "Relax Dad, It's Just the Kitchen" and future titles are available at the official Relax Dad web site, www.RelaxDad.com

Follow the author on Twitter @RelaxDadBook or on Facebook.

The author, Stan Reese, is also available as a motivational speaker. Contact him through RelaxDad.com

Made in the USA
Charleston, SC
23 April 2012